Reforming Federalism – Foreign Experiences for a Reform in Germany

Rechtspolitisches Symposium
Legal Policy Symposium

Herausgegeben im Institut für Rechtspolitik an der Universität Trier
von Bernd von Hoffmann und Gerhard Robbers

Band 3

PETER LANG
Frankfurt am Main · Berlin · Bern · Bruxelles · New York · Oxford · Wien

Gerhard Robbers (ed.)

Reforming Federalism – Foreign Experiences for a Reform in Germany

Reports of a Symposium held in Trier
on December 2nd to 4th, 2004

hosted by
the Institute for Legal Policy at the University of Trier
in Cooperation with the German Bundesrat

PETER LANG
Europäischer Verlag der Wissenschaften

Bibliographic Information published by Die Deutsche Bibliothek
Die Deutsche Bibliothek lists this publication in the Deutsche Nationalbibliografie; detailed bibliographic data is available in the internet at <http://dnb.ddb.de>.

ISSN 1610-8906
ISBN 3-631-54621-1
US-ISBN 0-8204-9815-7

www.peterlang.de

TABLE OF CONTENTS

PREFACE

The reform of federalism remains a predominant challenge in Germany. A major attempt to meet this challenge was the Commission on Federalism which started its sessions on 7 November 2003 and ended its work on 17 December 2004. Even though the Commission on Federalism has not submitted any formal suggestions its discussions and negotiations remain relevant. The Commission on Federalism has made visible possibilities of change.

Supporting the ongoing discussion about federalism in Germany it can be helpful to look beyond the borders. Federalism has been a remarkably successful model in structuring political rule. Many states have adopted this system. Federalism facilitates experiments in restructuring government, federalism eases cultural contradictions, and federalism facilitates maintaining regional identities. Federalism is an expression of the separation of powers and thus it is a guardian against the misuse of political rule. Federalism strengthens the ability to compete if a good balance is found between complexity and unity and to avoid that different powers blocade each other.

The contributions to the Trier Conference on Federalism from 2 to 4 December 2004 collected in this volume give an account of a broad range of experiences in reforming federalism in many countries of the world. These contributions represent a treasure of comparative constitutionalism.

The conference was organized by the Institute for Legal Policy at the University of Trier in cooperation with the German Bundesrat. It brought together leading scholars, administrative and political actors in the field of federalism. The cooperation of all contributors is gratefully acknowledged.

A special word of thanks goes to the Institute's staff for their contribution to the conference: Mr. Michael Blumenstock, Ms Julia Oppermann, Mr. Oliver Windgätter, Ms Maren Andres, Ms Julia Kugler, Mr. Nico Neukam, Mr. Marcel Nuys, Mr. Timo Rosenkranz, and Ms Claudia Lehnen.

Trier, Spring 2005

Prof. Dr. Gerhard Robbers

I. FEDERAL LEGISLATION

– BICAMERAL SYSTEMS IN COMPARISON –

Horst Risse

THE BUNDESRAT IN THE FEDERAL LEGISLATIVE PROCESS –

BICAMERALISM IN GERMANY

The political life in Germany is controlled not only by the federal level as the central authority, but also by the Länder, the Bundesrat being one of the key institutions in this framework. In comprehensive and intense consultations, the Parliamentary Council, which prepared the Basic Law of the Federal Republic of Germany after World War II, considered the question of how the participation of the Länder should be structured within a second parliamentary organ alongside the Bundestag. Among the models proposed was that of the US Senate, whose members are elected. Finally, a large majority formed in favour of Germany's traditional form of a Federal Council, in which the members come from the Länder governments.

This rather unique structure dates back to the Bismarck constitution of the German Empire of 1871 and the Weimar Constitution of 1919, both had comparable chambers. The Bundesrat is not a directly elected body. But Länder elections always are also indirect Bundesrat elections as they determine the Land government which then sends its members into the second federal house. The Länder representation there is neither proportional to the number of inhabitants nor equal like in the US Senate. But the number of votes and seats for the individual Land is calculated in a manner that works clearly in favour of the smaller entities.

I. The Bundesrat in the Legislative Procedure

The Bunderat is a federal organ. Article 50 of the Basic Law describes its status and functions:

> "The Länder shall participate through the Bundesrat in the legislative process and administration of the Federation and in matters concerning the European Union."

In the first place, the Bundesrat is a legislative organ. Its constitutional rank and political power comes from its influence in the federal legislative process.

Just like the Bundestag and the Federal Government, the Bundesrat has the right to introduce bills (legislative initiative). If, on the application of one or more Länder, the Bundesrat approves a bill of its own, then the bill is forwarded to the Federal Government for comment. As the next step, the Federal

Government is required to forward the bill – normally within six weeks – to the Bundestag. About 8% of all bills are initiated by the Bundesrat.

As a matter of fact, most bills are introduced by the Federal Government. The Bundesrat has the "first say" in the parliamentary treatment, since the Federal Government is required to submit its proposals directly to the Bundesrat for comment. The review and discussion of government proposals is one of the Bundesrat's primary functions. The Länder's experience putting laws into practice – they are responsible for the implementation of almost all of them – is incorporated into federal legislation in this "first reading." At this stage, in the Bundesrat committees the Länder governments conduct an intensive dialogue on specifics with the Federal Government. The Bundesrat's assessment of a bill is not binding, neither for the Federal Government nor the Bundestag. Then the Federal Government formulates its views in a "counter-statement." The bill, the Bundesrat's initial statement and the Federal Government's counter-statement are then sent to the Bundestag.

All bills approved by the Bundestag must be sent to the Bundesrat. In this "second reading" the Bundesrat has to come to a final decision on the bill. It will determine whether its statement from the "first reading" has been taken into account and whether the Bundestag made further changes during its deliberations. Bills initiated by the Bundestag, and which for this reason were not previously submitted to the Bundesrat for assessment, are subject to special scrutiny.

If the Bundesrat does not agree with the bill passed by the Bundestag, it can apply, within a period of three weeks, to the Mediation Committee composed of 16 members of the Bundestag and Bundesrat respectively. The Mediation Committee may present a compromise to both houses. The committee has gained growing influence in the last couple of years. Many important bills have been dealt within the Committee. There is hardly a major reform which is not discussed in the Mediation Committee. The Mediation Committee has worked rather effectively: It could achieve agreement in 88% of the cases it had been called upon.

The Bundesrat's political power in the legislative process depends on the contents of the individual bill. Two types of bills are distinguished: consent bills and objection bills. Unless the Basic Law provides otherwise, a bill is an objection bill. But there are about 50 provisions in the Basic Law stating the requirement of the Bundesrat's consent to a bill. These bills are deemed to have a special bearing on Länder interests. Among them, three cases are of particular importance:

- First of all bills that would change the constitution. They require Bundesrat's approval based on a two-thirds majority.
- Secondly, federal bills affecting the Länder tax revenue.
- Thirdly, and this is the most important group, bills that affect the administrative jurisdiction of the Länder.

In all these cases, it is important to note that the entire bill becomes a consent bill if it includes only one single provision which meets the criteria of the Basic Law for the requirement of the Bundesrat approval.

Obviously, the Bundesrat has a particularly strong position in connection with consent bills. About 53% of all bills are consent bills. They cannot become law unless the Bundesrat gives its expressed approval. In these cases Bundestag and Bundesrat are equal in their powers. If the Bundesrat refuses its consent, the Bundestag as well as the Federal Government also may refer the bill to the Mediation Committee. However, if the Bundesrat still refuses to give its approval, the bill fails. In political practice, this is a rather rare case: Only 2.1% of all consent bills have failed because the Bundesrat refused its consent.

In case of objection bills, the Bundesrat can file on objection within two weeks of the conclusion of mediation proceedings. This means that the Bundestag will have to subject the bill to another reading. If the Bundestag does not share the Bundesrat's reservations, it can override the objection with an absolute majority, in certain cases with a two-thirds majority. If the objection is overridden, the bill in question may be promulgated despite the Bundesrat's disapproval. Only 0.43% of all objection bills have failed at the end.

II. Assessment of the Bundesrat's Role

The participation of the Bundesrat in the legislative process of the Federation expresses both the distribution of power and the checks and balances in the German federal system. In fact, the Bundesrat is a most effective counterweight to the Federal Government and the majority fraction in the Bundestag: As it is one of the characteristic features of a parliamentary system of government that the majority in parliament and the government are politically linked, control in parliament is limited to what the opposition can do using its minority rights. But the Bundesrat majority is formed independently from federal elections, and so there is no guarantee of a majority for the Federal Government in this chamber. In the more recent history of the Federal Republic the Bundesrat has often been dominated by a political colour different from the

Federal Government. This was the case between 1969 and 1982 and again since 1990. But even if Bundestag and Bundesrat majorities are likeminded in terms of party politics, a Federal Government may well have its difficulties with the Bundesrat. Länder interests always remain an important element in the Bunderat decision making process.

In terms of statistic, Bundestag and Bundesrat seem to work together quite well. However, the statistic does not reveal the political impact of the high percentage of consent bills. In order to get its bills through the Federal Government and the Bundestag majority very often have to compromise with the Bundesrat majority. The Bundestag majority and its Federal Government hardly have a chance to put their political programme into legislative reality. The nation seems to be governed by an informal great coalition of all major political powers. Complex and time consuming negotiations in the Mediation Committee often end up in compromise solutions on the level of a rather small common denominator. Furthermore, it is increasingly difficult for the voter to determine who is responsible for which political decision. Critics say: "As everybody seems to be in charge of everything, nobody is responsible for anything."

This analysis became rather popular at a time when Germany seemed to loose many of its long kept pool positions in the economic field. The federal system, with the Bundesrat as one of its keystones, was considered to be the reason, or at least one major reason, for slow and unsubstantial political decisions.

III. Current Attempts for Reform

Though the analysis summarised above is perhaps not as convincing as it seems at the first glace, it has been the starting point for the idea to come to a general reform of the federal system in Germany, including German bicameralism. In November 2003 Bundestag and Bundesrat founded the Joint Commission on the Modernisation of the Federal Order. Among other questions, one of the key issues of the commission's work was the participation of the Länder in the federal legislative process.

On a rather early stage of the deliberations, the Commission reached consensus that the number of federal bills requiring the Bundesrat's approval should be reduced substantially. About 50% of all consent bills need the Bundesrat's approval because they contain provisions on the Länder administrative procedure or the establishment of their relevant public authorities. Art. 84 sec. 1 of the Basic Law stipulates the requirement of the Bundesrat's approval for such bills. It is obvious that it would contribute substantially to the work of the Commission if this provision could be eliminated as a source of consent bills.

In fact, it is very likely that the Commission can come to an agreement in this respect. The solution discussed will keep the Federation's competence to regulated Länder administrative procedures and the establishment of public authorities but the Länder will get the right to deviate from the Federal law in these matters. On the other hand, such bills will no more need the Bundesrat's consent.

It goes without saying that such a reform would alter dramatically the equilibrium of power between federal and Länder levels, Bundestag and Bundesrat, and Federal Government and opposition. Obviously, it can only be one part of a larger package of changes in the overall architecture of German federalism. The general idea is to compensate the Länder for their loss of influence in the federal legislative process by shifting certain legislative competencies to the Länder themselves.

In the context of bicameralism, however, probably there will be only one aspect of compensation. The Länder have claimed that Art. 84 sec. 1 BL, though it was meant to protect their executive powers and competencies, in political practice often served as a tool to control and limit financial burdens put upon the Länder budgets by federal laws. The Basic Law stipulates that the level of state which is responsible for the implementation of a law has to bear the costs (Art. 104a sec. 1 BL). As the implementation of federal laws normally is vested in the Länder, they have to cover the related expenses. Expensive federal laws usually contain some provisions on administrative procedure so that Art. 84 sec. 1 BL normally makes them consent bills. As soon as Art. 84 sec. 1 BL will be changed in the way described above, it can no more be used to protect the Länder budgets from a too generous federal legislator.

It is generally accepted in the Commission that federal laws putting severe financial burdens upon the Länder should require the Bundesrat's consent. The Commission is currently seeking for a suitable clause for such a consent requirement.

This is a very difficult task in political and technical terms. The wording of the new consent requirement clause must cover grave financial burdens for the Länder in a reliable way. Furthermore, in the legislative process it is essential to be sure whether the conditions stipulated in the clause are met or not. As it is often very difficult to anticipate the costs of a new piece of legislation it is doubtful whether a solution can be found by establishing a threshold of an absolute amount in Euro or a percentage of the Länder budgets. On the other hand, there is consensus that the new consent requirement must not be construed in a way which would roll back the reduction of consent bills achieved by changing Art. 84 sec. 1 BL. Thus, a bill causing only minor additional expenses for the Länder should not require the Bundesrat's consent. One possible way to solve the problem might be to make a bill a consent bill if it stipulates a legal claim of private persons against the state for financial assistance (e.g. welfare, unemployment benefits, scholarships) or public services (e.g. child day-care, legal consultation service). Often, such bills are the most expensive pieces of legislation. But the Länder doubt whether a consent requirement of that kind would offer sufficient protection for them.

IV. The Future of German Bicameralism

Though the structure of the Bundesrat as chamber of the Länder governments and the legislative procedure as such are not part of the current debate in Germany it is very likely that the ongoing reform of the federal system will have a great impact on German bicameralism. The number of consent bills will be reduced considerably. The Bundestag majority and the Federal Government will have a much better chance to put their legislative programme into reality without the interference of an often "hostile" Bundesrat.

De constitutione lata, the Bundesrat is one of the more powerful second chambers in the world. It was not quite meant that way because when the Basic Law was drafted, the Parliamentary Council estimated that only about 10% of all federal bills would be consent bills. As pointed out, that rate is well over 50% now. After the reform we might end up at about one third of all federal bills. The political power of the future Bundesrat will be concentrated in financial matters. Perhaps, its role as a watchdog for the Länder budgets will be even stronger than now. But in all other matters the position of the Bundestag in the bicameral system will become stronger.

André Alen and Koen Muylle

THE BELGIAN SENATE IN A FEDERAL STATE – ORIGINS, PRACTICE AND REFORMS –

I. The Origins of the Belgian Senate: From an Aristocratic Chamber to an Assembly to Improve the Quality of Legislation[1]

Since its inception, in 1831, Belgium has always had a bicameral parliamentary system. Parliament consists of two assemblies, the House of Representatives and the Senate, which are independent one from another and which both represent the Nation.

Originally, the Senate was to be *a conservative counterweight* against the House of Representatives, that counted more middle class members, as one did not have to pay any taxes to be eligible to the House[2]. This idea was reflected mainly in the Senate's composition. To be eligible for the Senate, one had to pay at least 1000 guilders in direct taxes, an enormous amount of money at that time, and to be at least 40 years old. Moreover, senators were not entitled to any pay or allowance. Because of these eligibility requirements, only the aristocracy and major landowners could sit in the upper house. In 1840, only 668 persons met these criteria, in 1870 only 826. In 1848, 63 percent of the members belonged to the nobility. It was argued that the Senate was to be an instrument to ensure the government's stability and to prevent the House of Representatives from taking ill-considered and rapid decisions. In order to enable the Senate to check the House, both assemblies had almost identical competences.

However, over time the composition of the Senate gradually changed with *the democratisation process*. The 1893 Constitutional Reform introduced *sénateurs provinciaux* ("provincial" senators), i.e. senators appointed by the provincial councils, to whom the high tax requirement to be eligible to the Senate did not apply. Moreover, the amount of taxes one had to pay to be eli-

---

1 On the history of the Senate: see De Geschiedenis van de Belgische Senaat, Tielt, Lannoo, 1999. See also *Stengers, J.*, 'Les caractères généraux de l'évolution du Sénat depuis 1831', in: La réforme du Sénat, Brussels, Bruylant, 1990, 11-43.

2 On the choice of the *National Congress* in 1830 to have a Senate: see *Stevens, F.*, "Een belangrijke faze in de wordingsgeschiedenis van de Belgische Grondwet: de optie voor een tweekamerstelsel", Belgisch tijdschrift voor de nieuwste geschiedenis, 1981, 641-661.

gible for direct election as senator was reduced by almost fifty percent. The 1921 Constitutional Reform introduced the *sénateurs cooptés* ("co-opted" senators, i.e. senators chosen by the directly elected and by the provincial senators), and replaced the excessive tax requirement to be directly eligible for the Senate by a long list of 21 categories of eligible persons, based on their merits or their taxable income[3]. As almost anyone was able to enter into at least one of these 21 categories, the Senate thus became a second Chamber elected by the people similar to the House of Representatives. The Belgian parliamentary system hence evolved, as in other countries, into an undifferentiated and egalitarian bicameral system. The two Chambers had almost an identical profile, both in terms of composition[4] and in terms of responsibilities, each in turn performing the same work. In this new framework, the Senate received a new, less political and more technical, role[5]: it was to be an instrument to improve the quality of legislation.

II. The 1993-1995 Constitutional Reform[6] – The Dual Role of the Senate[7]

1. The 1993-1995 constitutional reform and the reform of the senate

On 5 May 1993, Belgian federal Parliament went through the most significant reform in its history. Its composition, its competences and its operations were thoroughly revised. *Two considerations* explained this reform: on the one hand, the federalisation process of the Belgian State; on the other hand, the increasing discontent with the bicameral system as it existed at that time.

3 See *Miroir, A./Quertainmont, Ph.*, "L'évolution des conditions d'éligibilité des sénateurs", in: Présence du droit public et des droits de l'homme. Mélanges offerts à Jacques Velu, Brussels, Bruylant, 1992, 475-493.

4 The sole difference between the eligibility requirements for the House and for the Senate, was that one had to be at least 40 years old to be eligible for the Senate and 25 years old to be eligible in the House.

5 *Leemans, E.*, "Het tweekamerstelsel in een nieuw perspectief", in: *Alen, A./ Suetens, L.P.* (eds.), Zeven knelpunten na zeven jaar staatshervorming, Brussels, Story-Scientia, 1988, (363) 370-371.

6 For a general overview of this reform, see: *Alen, A./Suetens, L.P.* (eds.), Het federale België na de vierde Staatshervorming, Bruges, Die Keure, 1993. See also Les réformes institutionnelles de 1993. Vers un fédéralisme achevé?, Brussels, Bruylant, 1994.

7 The 1993 amendments to the Constitution became operative on 21 May 1995, when the Senate in its new form was elected for the first time.

The ongoing federalisation process of the Belgian State[8] can, first of all, explain the 1993 reform of the Senate and of the federal Parliament. For the past thirty years, the unitary Belgian State has slowly changed into a federal State. Federated entities have been created which have gradually acquired ever-broader autonomy. While most federal States are built by association, summarised by the Latin maxim *e diversitate unitas*, federal Belgium was born of dissociation. Federalism is operating centrifugally[9]. Since 1993, Article 1 of the Belgian Constitution states that "Belgium is a federal State, constituted of communities and regions." The Belgian federal State is thus composed of two types of federated entities which overlap on the same territory. Belgium counts three communities: the Flemish (Dutch-speaking) Community, the (Walloon or) French(-speaking) Community and the German-speaking Community. Each community has responsibility for everything with regard to education and culture in the broadest sense. Belgium also includes three regions – the Flemish Region, the Walloon Region and the Brussels-Capital Region – whose responsibilities cover primarily the socio-economic sphere.

The federalisation process had two effects on the federal Parliament's composition.

On the one hand, in 1995, when the Parliaments of the federated entities were to be directly elected for the first time, the number of political officeholders would increase considerably[10]. Therefore, the number of members of the federal Parliament had to be reduced significantly. The number of members of the House of Representatives was brought from 212 to 150, the number of senators from 184 to 71 elected members.

On the other hand, in federal States the participation principle requires that the federated entities are able to take part in the federal law-making process, or at least in amendments to the Constitution or to Acts that directly concern the federated entities. It was therefore necessary to ensure that the federated entities were represented in the federal Parliament. The Senate thus became, at

---

8 See *Alen, A./Ergec, R.*, Federal Belgium after the Fourth State Reform of 1993, Brussels, Belgian Ministry of Foreign Affairs, Foreign Trade and Cooperation for Development, 1998 (2nd ed.).

9 See *Alen, A.*, Der Föderalstaat Belgien. Nationalismus – Föderalismus – Demokratie, Schriftenreihe der Europäischen Zentrums für Föderalismus – Forschung, Band 4, Baden-Baden, Nomos Verlagsgesellschaft, 1995, 40-42.

10 Before the generalisation of the direct election of the Parliaments of the federated entities in 1993, there were already almost 500 members of Parliament (the House of Representatives (212), the Senate (184), the Council of the German-speaking Community (25) and the Council of the Brussels-Capital Region (75).

least in part, a chamber that serves as a meeting place for the federated entities.

Another consideration contributed to the reform of the federal Parliament. As we explained, after the 1921 Constitutional Reform, the two chambers of the federal Parliament were very similar, both in terms of their composition and in terms of their responsibilities, each of them performing in turn exactly the same work. Moreover, the way parliamentary work was organised was the source of slowness and of sterile duplication. It was necessary to make the federal Parliament a modern and effective institution. The reform of 5 May 1993 has endeavoured to achieve that goal by rationalising the legislative procedure.

2. *The 1993-1995 reform of the senate: new composition and new division of competences*[11]

The main feature of *the new composition* of the Senate[12] is the introduction of representatives of the federated entities (the *sénateurs de communauté* or "community senators"). As we have already indicated, it was important for the federated entities to be represented as such in the federal Parliament and that they thereby participate in the federal law-making process.

Out of a total of 71 senators[13], 21 *sénateurs de communauté* ("community senators") are designated by the Parliaments of the three communities from among their members: 10 by the Parliament of the Flemish Community, 10 by the Parliament of the French Community and one by the Parliament of the German-speaking Community. Since they remain members of the Parliament that designated them, these senators perform a dual function, sitting both at the federal level and at the level of the federated entities. As, apart from the German Community senator, the members of the Flemish Parliament and of the

---

11 See, amongst others: *Suetens, L.P.*, "Purpose and functioning of the Senate in Belgium", in: *de Villiers, B./Delmartino, F./Alen, A.* (eds.), Institutional development in divided societies, Pretoria, HSRC Printers, 1998, 231-251.

12 Article 67 of the Constitution. For more details: see *Van Nieuwenhove, J.*, "De samenstelling van het federale Parlement", in: *Van der Hulst, M./Veny, L.* (eds.), Parlementair Recht. Commentaar en Teksten, Ghent, Mys & Breesch, 1998, A.2.2.1., 1-58.

13 Besides the 71 elected senators, there are, since 1831, also senators by right, i.e. the King's children that are 18 years old (Article 72 of the Constitution). At present, the Senate counts three senators by right: H.R.H. Prince Philippe, heir to the Throne, H.R.H. Princess Astrid and H.R.H. Prince Laurent.

Parliament of the French Community are also member of a regional Parliament, the regions are thus also indirectly represented in the Senate.

The remaining fifty senators belong to two categories: two electoral colleges elect forty senators: the Flemish or Dutch college directly elects 25 senators and the French college directly elects 15 senators. Secondly, the Senate also counts 10 co-opted senators, six of whom are designated by all of the other Dutch-speaking senators, and four by the French-speaking senators. While the allocation of seats for those two categories is based on the population numbers of the two main communities, there is parity between the Flemish and the French community senators.

The two main *missions* of the reformed Senate[14] are to be, on the one hand, a meeting place of the federal and federated authorities, and, on the other hand, a *Chambre de réflexion* ("Chamber for reflection"). The Senate was to guarantee the quality of legislation.

Since the "community senators" remain members of the Community Parliament that appoints them, and as some of them are also member of a regional assembly, these senators hold two or three offices. They are a direct link between the federal Parliament and the assemblies of the federated entities. They can monitor the actions of both the federal and federated governments. They can defend the interests of the federated entities at the federal level, and vice versa. They can assure, at least in theory, that actions undertaken at one level don't interfere with actions at the other level.

The second mission explains the new division of competences between the House of Representatives and the Senate, which is to prevent duplication and to enhance the efficiency of the parliamentary procedure.

Instead of an integral bicameral system, whereby both chambers of Parliament have to agree on an identical text, the Constitution now distinguishes between three types of laws. For all laws which involve the structure of the State and its institutions, the House of Representatives and the Senate remain competent on an equal footing[15]. This means that in these matters, legislative bills are passed only if both chambers reach an agreement on an identical text. The

---

14 For more details on the competences of the Senate: see *Vandernacht, P./ Van Nieuwenhove, J.*, "De nieuwe federale wetgevende procedure", in: *Leus, K./Veny, L.* (eds.), Het federale België in de praktijk, Bruges, Die Keure, 1996, 91-148 and "La réforme des assemblées législatives à la lumière des révisions constitutionnelles de 1993", Revue belge de droit constitutionnel, 1994, 65-97.

15 For a complete list of subject matters for which integral bicameralism applies: see Article 77 of the Constitution.

same holds, of course, for the Constitution[16]. It should also be noted that the Constitution has remained an exclusively federal matter, but the "community senators" warrant the participation of the federated entities in its revision and in the establishment of federal legislation governing their status. International treaties are also subject to approval by the two chambers[17].

For all other areas, the Constitution chose for a form of restricted bicameralism. Intervention by the Senate is optional and the House of Representatives is entitled to the last word. Once the House has adopted a bill, the Senate only examines it if 15 senators request to do so. The Senate can amend the bill within 60 days and send it back to the House, which then reviews it again. The number of *navettes* ("shuttles") between the two chambers is limited and at the end the House of Representatives prevails[18].

In a limited number of special areas[19], i.e. legislation on civil and criminal liability for federal ministers, approval of federal State budgets and accounts, the establishment of contingent of the army, as well as granting naturalisation, only the House has legislative power, to the exclusion of the Senate. In practice, however, most of these Acts have no normative content.

Moreover, political control of the federal government and of public finances was attributed exclusively to the House of Representatives.

During the 1999-2003 term, out of a total of 433 bills, which the House transmitted to the Senate, 334 bills were optional bicameral bills and 99 bills were integral bicameral bills. Thus 22.9 percent of the bills the House submitted to the Senate were integral bicameral bills; 77.1 percent of the bills that the Senate received from the House were optional bicameral bills, i.e. bills it did not necessarily have to examine. As we will explain below, in about 45 percent of the cases, it decided not to do so. In the remaining 55 percent, at least 15 senators asked the Senate to examine the bill.

---

16 The procedure to amend the Constitution is laid down in the Articles 195 to 198 of the Constitution.

17 The Senate enjoys a certain priority as far as the approval of international treaties is concerned, as approval bills have to be tabled first in that assembly (Article 75, section 3 of the Constitution).

18 Articles 78 and 79 of the Constitution.

19 Article 74 of the Constitution.

Ratio Optional/Integral Bills submitted by the House to the Senate

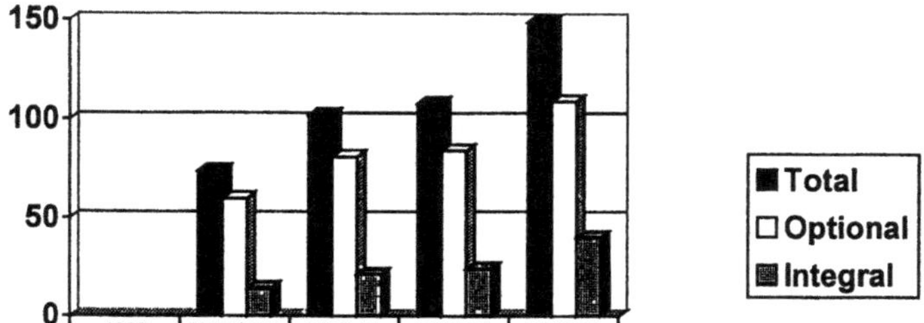

	1999	1999-2000	2000-01	2001-02	2002-03
Total	-	74	102	108	149
Optional	-	60	81	84	109
Integral	-	14	21	24	40

3. *An assessment of the reform of the senate*

How to assess the 1993-1995 Constitutional Reform ten years after it became operative? The appraisal has to be done taking into account the two objectives of the reform of the Senate, i.e. enhance its role as a federal assembly and improve the division of competences between the House and the Senate, turning the latter into a *Chambre de réflexion*.

a) The Senate as a federal assembly

As far as the *composition* of the Senate is concerned, as we explained above, the "community senators" are to represent the federated entities.

For several reasons, that objective has not been met[20].

First of all, the number of "community senators" is limited. They are only 21, out of 71 elected members. This is only 30 percent of the total number of senators.

Moreover, to ensure that the majority in the Senate is the same as in the House, the allocation of seats is not based on the result of the elections for the Community Parliaments, but on those for the directly elected senators[21]. To determine which party is entitled to a seat of "community senator", one applies

20 *Alen, A.*, "La nécessité d'un Sénat comme seconde chambre des États et comme garant de la qualité de la législation", in: Quelles réformes pour le Sénat ?, Brussels, Bruylant, 2002, 20-23.

21 Article 68, section 1, of the Constitution and Article 211, section 2 of the Electoral Code.

the D'hondt system to the results of the elections for, on the one hand, the 25 senators directly elected by the Flemish electoral college and, on the other hand, the 15 senators directly elected by the French electoral college. The office of "community senator" only lasts for, in principle, four years, i.e. the term for which the federal Parliament is elected, while the Community Parliaments are elected for a fixed term of five years. Hence, when there are elections for the Community Parliaments during the term of the Senate, they will, in principle, not affect the political division of seats in the Senate[22].

Finally, apart from the German Community senator, who is elected by the majority of the Parliament of the German-speaking Community, the other "community senators" are chosen by their respective political group in the Flemish Parliament or the Parliament of the French Community[23]. Although the Constitution provides that the "community senators" are appointed by their respective Community Parliament, in practice the assembly merely ratifies the choices of the political groups.

In the Senate, "community senators" are rarely treated as such. They join the political group on whose list they are elected. They do not enjoy any specific prerogatives. Moreover, in their Community Parliament, the situation is much the same: the "community senators" are not granted a special role or mission.

Because of all these elements, "community senators" do not so much act as representatives of their federated entity, but rather as representatives of the political parties that appoint them[24].

A final flaw concerns the fact that only the communities are as such represented in the Senate. There are no representatives of the regions. This is partly resolved by the fact that the members of the Community Parliaments are at the same time member of a regional Parliament. Hence, they are also able to voice the concerns of the region whereto they belong in the Senate.

As far as the Senate's *competences* are concerned, the presence of the "community senators" in the Senate was supposed to enable the federated entities to take part in the federal law-making process, especially for those Acts that are of direct concern to them, i.e. legislation governing their status. "Community senators" were able to play this role in specific areas. For instance, they had an

22 However, if a community senator fails to be reelected as a member of his Community Parliament, he will have to be replaced in the Senate by another member belonging to the same political group.

23 See Article 211, section 4 of the Electoral Code.

24 *Vanhee, D.*, "De rol van de Vlaamse gemeenschapssenatoren in de Belgische federale staatsstructuur tijdens de legislatuur 1995-1999", Res Publica, 2004, 122-141.

important input in a working group on mobility policy: as this is also in part a regional matter, they had a lot to contribute because of their expertise within their regional Parliament. The same was the case when the Senate's Institutional Affairs Committee decided to assess Belgium's federal structures[25].

The presence of the "community senators" and the idea that the federated entities should thus be able to take part in the development of federal legislation that is important to them, explain that the Senate has full jurisdiction as far as amendments to the Constitution are concerned, as well for special majority laws.

For the special majority laws, each assembly is divided into a Dutch and a French linguistic group[26]. In the Senate, the 25 senators directly elected by the Dutch electoral college, the 10 senators designated by the Flemish Parliament and the 6 Dutch-speaking co-opted senators make up the Dutch linguistic group, in total 41 senators. The 15 senators directly elected by the French electoral college, the 10 senators designated by the Parliament of the French Community and the 4 French-speaking co-opted senators make up the French linguistic group, in total 29 senators[27]. The senator designated by the Parliament of the German-speaking Community, as well as the senators by right are not part of any linguistic group. The special majority laws require, in each of the chambers of the federal Parliament, besides a two-third majority overall, a majority within each linguistic group[28].

It should be pointed out that, although the jurisdiction of the Senate and the continued integral bicameralism for amendments to the Constitution, special majority laws and other laws are based *inter alia* on the presence of "community senators", those senators are not granted specific prerogatives in the adoption of those Acts. The linguistic groups are much more important.

As far as optional bicameral bills are concerned, which the Senate only examines if at least fifteen of its members request to do so, "community senators" do not enjoy special prerogatives neither. Although they may support a request to examine a bill, and may contribute to the debate, the "community senators" of one community are not sufficient in number to oblige the Senate to examine an optional bicameral bill.

---

25 See the report of the Senate's Institutional Affairs Committee, Assessment of the operation of the new federal structure, Parliamentary Documents Senate, 1998-1999, n° 1-1333/1 (available on http://www.senate.be).

26 Article 43 of the Constitution.

27 Article 43, section 2, of the Constitution. See also Article 17 of the Senate's Rules of Procedure.

28 Article 4, section 3 of the Constitution.

The Senate also plays a role in the settlement of "conflicts of interest" between the federal and federated assemblies[29]. When an assembly considers that a bill submitted in another assembly could seriously damage its interests, and the conflict cannot be settled by mutual arrangement, it calls upon the Senate to examine the conflict[30]. The Senate, however, only plays an advisory role. The final decision, taken by consensus, belongs to the "Concertation Committee", composed of representatives of the federal and federated governments. Moreover, even this "decision" is not binding. Conflicts of interest also often put "community senators" whom, at the level of the Community Parliament, voted in favour of the conflict, in a difficult position. It may occur that at the Senate's level, they suddenly will have to vote in favour of a motion that considers that the interests of the assembly concerned are not seriously damaged.

Ratio Optional bills submitted/examined/amended

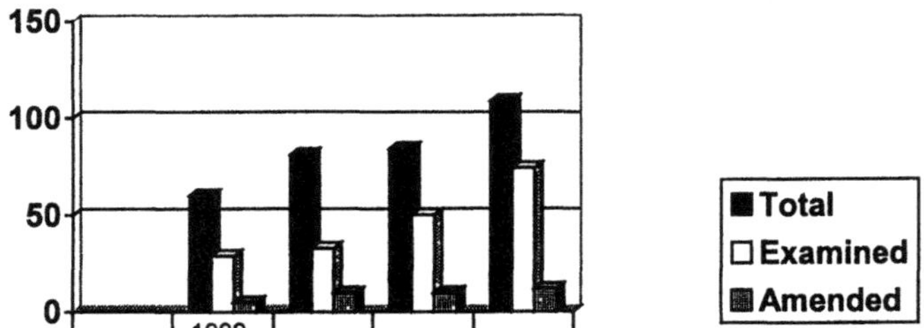

	1999	1999-2000	2000-01	2001-02	2002-03
Total	-	60	81	84	109
Examined	-	29	33	50	74
Amended	-	5	10	10	12

29 Article 143, section 2, of the Constitution and Article 32 of the Ordinary Institutional Reform Act of 9 August 1980. For more details: see *Van der Biesen, G.*, "De voorkoming en regeling van belangenconflicten tussen wetgevende vergaderingen", in: *Van der Hulst, M./Veny, L.* (eds.), Parlementair Recht. Commentaar en Teksten, Ghent, Mys & Breesch, 2000, B.2.5.3.6., 1-145.

30 Except if either the House or the Senate considers that a bill examined by a community or regional assembly could seriously damage its interests. In that case, the conflict immediately goes to the Concertation Committee.

b) *The Senate as a Chambre de réflexion*

The reformed Senate was also to be a *Chambre de réflexion*, a guarantee for the quality of legislation. As the Senate does not have to examine all the bills adopted by the House, it was thought that the Second Chamber would have more time available to examine some topics thoroughly.

In practice, the Senate was in part able to play this role. Last term, it spent for instance almost two years in examining a bill on euthanasia and focused on bio-ethical topics. This term, the Senate, and in particular its legal affairs committee, drew it upon itself to examine the revision of two codes, i.e. the Code on Private International Law[31] and the Code on Criminal Procedure[32]. Moreover, the figures show that the Senate does not examine all optional bicameral bills: only in 55 percent of the cases, 15 senators or more request to examine an optional bicameral bill.

During the 1999-2003 term, the House submitted 334 optional bicameral bills to the Senate. In 186 cases, 15 senators or more asked to examine the bill concerned[33]. Out of these 186 bills, the Senate decided to amend 36[34] of them, which means that it amended 19.3 percent of the optional bicameral bills submitted by the House and examined by the Senate[35]. In most of the cases, the amendments by the Senate are well received by the House.

---

31 Bill containing a Code on Private International Law, Parliamentary Documents Senate, 2003, n° 3-27/1 ff. This Bill became the Act of 16 July 2004 containing a Code on Private International Law, published in the Belgisch Staatsblad-Moniteur belge of 27 July 2004.

32 Bill containing a Code on Criminal Procedure, Parliamentary Documents Senate, 2003-2004, n° 3-450/1 ff. This bill is still debated in the Senate at the time of writing.

33 This was a serious increase compared to the 1995-1999 term, when the House submitted 315 optional bicameral bills to the Senate, and the Senate decided to examine 126 (or 40 percent) of them. 189 optional bicameral bills submitted by the House were thus not examined.

34 The Senate amended twice one and the same bill (bill to amend the legislation concerning the protection of the patrimonium of persons who because of physicial or mental reasons are unable to administer their own goods, *Parliamentary Documents* Senate, 2001-2002, n° 2-1078/1), which explains why the total number (36) is lower than the sum of each year separately (5+10+10+12=37).

35 Although the total number of optional bicameral bills examined by the Senate increased considerably compared to the 1995-1999 term, the total number of amended bills was almost the same: 34. This means that the percentage of optional bicameral bills that the Senate amended decreased from 27 percent to 19.3 percent. In other words, the Senate decided to examine more, but to amend less.

Fate of the optional bicameral bills amended by the Senate[36]	
Accepted by the House	21
Cross-amended[37]	11
Amendment rejected[38]	1
Fallen[39]	3
Total	36

Nevertheless, both in the Senate's composition and in its proceedings, there are a number of shortcomings vis-à-vis the aim of a Senate as *Chambre de réflexion*.

As far as the Senate's *composition* is concerned, there are problems with all three of the categories of senators.

First of all, the directly elected senators are elected in three very large constituencies: one that corresponds with almost the whole of the Flemish Region, one that corresponds with the Walloon Region, and finally the constituency of Brussels-Halle-Vilvoorde. These very large constituencies tend to draw the candidatures of the most important politicians (ministers or party chairmen). But their profile does not really fit the needs of an assembly that wants to focus on legislation in order to enhance its quality, as they do not have the time, nor the interest in legislative work.

A similar problem arises with the "community senators." As we explained, they are at the same time member of their Community Parliament and of the Senate (the so-called "double mandate"). However, each mandate is in itself very time consuming and members complain that it is very difficult for them to fulfill both offices to their full satisfaction. Most members tend to choose by giving priority to either the Senate or their Community Parliament. In the latter case, this harms of course the legislative work in the Senate.

36 For the 1999-2003 term. The numbers for the 1995-1999 term are pretty similar: out of the 34 amended bills, the House accepted 20 without any changes, cross amended 13 bills and rejected in one case the amendment adopted by the Senate.

37 Which means that the House made other amendments to the bill than those adopted by the Senate. In all but one of these cases, the bills were consequently adopted by the Senate.

38 Which means that the House returned to the text it adopted before submitting it to the Senate. The bill is subsequently sent to the King for approval (which is in principle always granted) and publication.

39 As a result of the dissolution of the House and the Senate in 2003.

Finally, the "co-opted senators" in theory fit very well into the idea of a Senate as guarantee of the quality of legislation. Originally, this category was created in 1921 to enable the Senate to call upon highly competent men and women (university professors, businessmen, etc.), who would not be willing to submit themselves to the electoral competition. In practice, however, the possibility to co-opt senators has become a tool to enable candidates who failed to be directly elected nevertheless to obtain a seat in Parliament.

Also in terms of the Senate's *competences and procedure*, there are a number of difficulties in respect of the Senate's role as guarantee for the quality of legislation.

As we explained above, the Constitution distinguishes between integral bicameralism, optional bicameralism and monocameralism. It is, however, not always easy to know if a given subject-matter belongs to one or the other procedure, which may cause a conflict between the House and the Senate to know what procedure is to be applied. A joint committee[40], which consists of 22 members of both chambers, has to settle these conflicts, which do not enter within the jurisdiction of the courts, including the Constitutional Court. Moreover, some bills deal with subject matters that are to be dealt with using in part the integral bicameral procedure, and in part the optional bicameral procedure. Thus, it happens that one has to table two bills, using a different procedure, to legislate in a given area. Indeed, if a bill dealing with a subject matter which is governed by the optional bicameral procedure contains one or more provisions for which the integral bicameral procedure applies (e.g. a provision concerning the jurisdiction of the courts), it has to be split[41].

Another difficulty concerns the optional bicameral procedure: when the Senate decides to examine a bill adopted by the House, it only has a limited time (in principle 60 days) to do so. This idea seems hardly compatible with the idea of

---

40 Article 82 of the Constitution and the April 6, 1995 Act on the creation of the Parliamentary Concertation Committee. See *Van der Hulst, M./Veny, L.*, "De parlementaire overlegcommissie", in: *Van der Hulst, M./Veny, L.* (eds.), Parlementair Recht. Commentaar en Teksten, Ghent, Mys & Breesch, A.2.3., 1-53.

41 See *Van der Hulst, M.*, "De nieuwe wetgevingsprocedure in de praktijk: over mengen en splitsen", Tijdschrift voor Bestuurswetenschappen en Publiek Recht, 1997, 589-597. See also the report of the Senate's Institutional Affairs Committee, Assessment of the operation of the new federal structure, Parliamentary Documents Senate, 1998-1999, n° 1-1333/1, 836. For a more general appraisal of the legislative procedure after the 1993-1995 Constitutional Reform became operative: see *Deltour, J./ Van Nieuwenhove, J./Wouters, M.*, "Vijf jaar nieuwe wetgevingsprocedure", Tijdschrift voor Wetgeving, 2000, 96-124 and 260-281.

a Senate as a *Chambre de réflexion*, i.e. an assembly which has more time available to examine important bills.

III. Future Reforms

On April 26, 2002, the federal government agreed on a plan to reform once more the Senate[42]. This reform should be implemented during the present term of Parliament.

According to the agreement of April 26, 2002, the role of the Senate as a chamber where the communities and the regions meet would be reinforced. The Senate would become an assembly composed of 35 Dutch-speaking representatives and 35 French-speaking representatives designated by the Flemish and French Community Parliament respectively, with a guaranteed representation of the (regional) Brussels-Capital Parliament and one representative from the German-speaking Community.

The Community Parliaments would have to choose at least 30 representatives among their members and among the members of their government. This would enable each of them to choose five "outsiders", comparable to the co-opted senators. The way the seats would be allocated – whether the majority of the Community Parliament would be entitled to all the seats, whether the allocation would reflect the division of seats in the Community Parliament concerned or in the one in the House of Representatives – has so far not been determined. The same applies to the term of the mandate of these senators: five years, as the Community Parliaments, or four years as the House? However, these are crucial elements to know whether possibly the Senate would have a different majority from the one in the House.

As before, the Senate would be competent, on equal terms with the House, for amending the Constitution and for adopting special majority laws and other State reform laws. The Senate would also have jurisdiction to approve mixed treaties (that concern subject-matters for which not only the federal State but also the communities and/or regions have jurisdiction) and multilateral cooperation agreements, the other Parliaments having the right to examine these treaties and agreements upon simple request.

As far as other bills adopted by the House are concerned, the Senate would only examine them if a majority within a linguistic group requests to do so.

42 On this agreement: see *Vuye, H./Stangherlin, K.*, "Vers une sixième réforme de l'État? Réflexions sur l'accord dit de renouveau politique du 26 avril 2002", Chroniques de droit public, 2002, 263-282.

The Senate would be able to table amendments on House bills if they are agreed to by a majority within both linguistic groups. The House would have the final word whether or not to agree to these amendments. The Senate would also have the right to table a bill in the House and to address recommendations to the House.

The implementation of this reform would require major changes to the Constitution. Before the federal elections of May 18, 2003, Parliament has initiated the procedure enabling the present Parliament to adopt these changes by indicating which articles are subject to change in the present term. Almost all constitutional provisions with regard to the Senate are up for revision[43]. However, the adoption of these amendments to the Constitution requires a two-third majority in both the House and Senate.

At present, it is hard to foresee whether these reform plans will become reality. The declaration of the federal government of October 12, 2004[44] referred all outstanding issues to an institutional Forum, an *ad hoc* body that consists of representatives of the federal government, the regions and the communities, as well as a limited number of members of the House and of the Senate. Since its creation, this body has only met once. It does not have a firm timetable indicating by what time the negotiators should come to an agreement. It is thus possible that the agreement of April 26, 2002 will never be implemented, especially because the Senate would have to agree – with a two-third majority – to the necessary amendments to the Constitution.

IV. Final Remarks and Conclusions

Belgium had from 1831 until 1995 an integral bicameral system, in which both chambers of Parliament had, since the democratisation-process in 1921, an almost identical composition, and also almost identical competences.

The waste of time that this system caused, e.g. because of the *navettes* ("shuttles") of bills between both chambers, and, especially, the transformation of Belgium from a decentralised unitary State into a federal State, resulted in the 1993-1995 Constitutional Reform, which gave the Senate a dual role. On the one hand, the Senate was to become a meeting place of the federated entities. The "community senators" are to represent the interests of the federated enti-

43 Declaration to amend the Constitution of 9 April 2003, Belgisch Staatsblad-Moniteur belge, 10 April 2003 (2nd ed.).

44 Available on the internet at http://premier.fgov.be/nl/politics/20041012-pol-declar-nl.pdf.

ties at the federal level, and to enable them to take part in the federal law-making process. On the other hand, as a *Chambre de réflexion*, the Senate has an important role to play to improve the quality of legislation.

Although the Senate has in part succeeded in this dual role, we have pointed out a number of flaws, both in its composition and in its competences.

These shortcomings have led to new reform plans, in which the Senate would become, as in other federal States, a "Second Chamber of States." The Senate would consist (almost) exclusively of representatives of the federated entities. In order to comply with the participation principle in a federal State, it would have an effective say – on an equal footing with the House of Representatives – in the revision of the federal Constitution and the federal legislation in matters directly affecting the interests of the federated entities.

The 2002 political agreement therefore has a strong federal logic. However, it completely abandons the idea that the Senate also has an important role to play as a guarantor of the quality of legislation. One thus has the impression that the possible criticisms that could be made against the present composition and competences are used in the 2002 political agreement to seriously tone down the optional bicameral system. Although the Senate has at several occasions improved legislation, we have the impression that the federal government considers the assembly as a burden. As far as the quality of bills is concerned, the 2002 political agreement provides for a second reading by a committee of the House. However, the experience with the – monocameral – Community and Regional Parliaments, where such a procedure already exists, has shown that it harms the quality of legislation. In our view[45], quality of legislation is of such importance, because it is not limited to merely legislative drafting: it requires legal certainty, foreseeability and accessibility of Acts of Parliament, requirements that according to the *Arbitragehof – Cour d'arbitrage* (the Belgian Constitutional Court) are essential for the rule of law[46].

Bogdanor wrote in this respect that "it is that legislation of a highly technical kind, such as emanates from the European Community, needs technically qualified legislators to appraise it. Here perhaps is a role for an upper house, composed not of professional politicians, and not too closely beholden to party. What is needed is perhaps more akin to a standing advisory committee

---

45 See *Alen, A.*, "La nécessité d'un Sénat comme seconde chambre des États et comme garant de la qualité de la législation", in: Quelles réformes pour le Sénat?, Brussels, Bruylant, 2002, 19-27.

46 See e.g. Arbitragehof-Cour d'arbitrage, Judgment n° 106/2004, 16 June 2004, Belgisch Staatsblad-Moniteur belge, 2 July 2004.

of experts, or a standing royal commission rather than a legislative chamber in the strict sense of the word"[47]. This statement fits very well into his general approach, according to which "the existence or absence of an upper house is not the crucial factor likely to determine the success of democratic government or its ability to secure constitutional protection. An upper house is a means rather than an end"[48]. The same author has also written: "Moreover, in modern democracies, party politics tends to prevent the upper house from acting as a genuine protector of states rights. (...). Upper houses in federal systems are as much party houses as they are state houses. Further, in federal states, it is the courts and inter-governmental forums, such as federal/provincial conferences, linking together the states and the federal government which play at least as important a role as protectors of states rights as the upper house"[49].

However, *Mastias* and *Grangé* opined: "second chambers have as objective, or as merit, to guarantee and to reassure", *inter alia* by "toning down, balancing and stabilising the powers" and by "guaranteeing pluralism"[50].

Some have nevertheless argued that bicameralism is not necessary in bipolar federal States[51]. Although one could be tempted to apply this statement to the Belgian federation – which is bipolar – we disagree with it, because in a federal monocameral system, the danger exists that federal Parliament rather represents the two communities than the nation as a whole. In the Belgian context, it does not seem a good idea to reduce the State and its institutions to the antagonism between its two principal communities[52]. There should also be an assembly that tries to overcome the bipolar nature of the State. It is therefore not a coincidence that almost all federations have bicameral legislatures[53]. In a federal State such as Belgium, the principle of participation justifies the exis-

---

47 *Bogdanor, V.*, "The problem of the upper house", in: *Blom, H.W./Blockmans, W.P./De Schepper, H.* (eds.), Bicameralisme. Tweekamerstelsel vroeger en nu, The Hague, Sdu Uitgeverij Koninginnengracht, 1992, 421.

48 *Ibidem.*

49 O.c., 416.

50 *Mastias, J./Grangé, J.* (eds.), Les secondes chambres du Parlement en Europe occidentale, Paris, Economica, 1987, 99.

51 *Herrero De Minon, M.*, "The passing of bicameralism", American Journal of Comparative Law, 1975, 241.

52 *Alen, A./Meersschaut, F.*, "Le bicaméralisme belge, de la voie unitaire à la voie fédérale", Administration Publique – Trimestriel, 1990, 159.

53 *Watts, R.L.*, Comparing Federal Systems, Montreal and Kingston, McGill-Queen's University Press, 1999 (2nd ed.), 92.

tence of a Senate. We therefore believe that Belgium needs a Senate, not only for this reason, but also to temper the House.

At a conference on future reforms of the Belgian Senate in November 2001, *Smith* argued persuasively that "the present Nordic system illustrates very well that the potential and real advantages of a bicameral system will only appear when the second chamber is composed along different lines than the first chamber. The second chamber has to have a specific character. Otherwise, a bicameral system does not make sense."[54] Taking into account the federal character of the Belgian State, the *composition* of the Senate thus has to be different from that of the House, whereby more co-opted and competent persons should be able to sit in the Senate, in order to assist Parliament, e.g. to implement European Community legislation. The *competences* of the Senate should also differ from those of the first chamber. In a federal State with a cabinet government, the government must be responsible to one chamber – the lower house – only[55]. However, the Senate has to have the same competences as the first chamber as far as amendments to the Constitution and State reform laws are concerned. Apart from that it should be a *Chambre de réflexion*, which contributes to the quality of legislation.

---

54 "Quelles réformes pour le Sénat? Suggestions de dix-huit constitutionnalistes", Brussels, Sénat de Belgique, Compte rendu, 12 November 2001, 30.

55 *Bogdanor, V.*, o.c., 415: 'In Australia, where (...) the Senate is able to reject supply, there is a very real conflict between federalism and the principle of cabinet government, entailing the responsibility of the government to the lower house'. See also *Watts, R.L.*, o.c., 96.

Beniamino Caravita di Toritto

BICAMERALISM IN ITALY: ITS PAST, PRESENT AND FUTURE OUTLOOK

I. The Past and Present of Bicameralism

The division of parliament into two distinct chambers (the bicameral system) is a feature common to many countries. However, it is rare for the two houses to be placed on the same level, to be elected in the same or very similar manner, and to have the same legislative functions, both in the legislative process and in relations with the government, and in its activities of scrutiny and control, as it is currently the case in Italy according to the model of "egalitarian" or "perfect" bicameralism. In fact, in most countries the two houses differ in investiture and functions, with the lower house almost always holding supremacy over the upper.

Historically, bicameralism has had four main tasks:

a) to balance the principle of sovereignty of the people with the principle of monarchical sovereignty; one chamber's representatives were nominated by the monarch and one was composed of popularly elected representatives (such is the bicameral system in United Kingdom and was in Italy under the Albertine Statute);
b) to afford fully integrated political representation, with a second chamber representing differing economic, social and cultural interests;
c) to act as a means of compensation and reflection, thus ensuring that power is not concentrated in one house and improving the legislative process;
d) to adapt to the territorial make-up of the state; this is the case of federal or regional states where a house representing the entire citizenry is flanked by a second house representing single federal entities.

In Italy the Constituent Assembly, established after World War II, opted for a second chamber (the Senate of the Republic) of reflection and compensation. The founding fathers introduced some corrections to ensure, on paper at least, that the second house would not be a mere duplicate of the first, in order to create a model of "perfect" bicameralism (with regard to powers), but not "egalitarian" (as regards its configuration). As with many other parts of the Italian constitution, the Constituent Assembly's decision on bicameralism was the result of a compromise. It was a compromise between those who wanted a unicameral system (Communist party, Socialist party, Partito d'azione, a left-radical small party) and those who wanted an imperfect bicameral system, with a second House representing segments of productive society (some Christian Democrats) or elected by the electoral majority system (Liberals) or representing the regions (Republicans). As it often happens with compromises, the result (bicameralism, but egalitarian and perfect, with two houses equally representative of the popular will and sharing the same functions) did not satisfy anyone, and, since then, the Italian bicameral system has been subject to frequent criticism and attempts to reform (which have, until now, all proven ineffective).

In practice, Italian bicameralism has warranted more negative criticism than positive. The second house has indeed played a role of reflection, or, as is often said, of "cooling", but it has also excessively lengthened the time needed to pass legislation. Moreover, within a form of parliamentary government like Italy's, the negative effects of perfect bicameralism on the stability of the government should not be underestimated. It is more difficult for the government to obtain the confidence of both houses (which may have different political composition) and to implement government policy with two actors than with just one. Moreover, the rules of procedure of each house are often very different, so much that one house may be more governable than the other.

In fact, the differences between the Chamber of Deputies and the Senate of the Republic, introduced by the Constituent Assembly, were of little significance and have become less so over the years to the point of loosing any political significance. The differences between the Chamber and Senate are:

a) the number of elected members; 630 deputies in the Chamber, 315 in the Senate. By reducing the number of Senate members, the Constituent Assembly intended to make its work easier and quicken the decision making process;
b) the age difference of the electorate (persons 18 years or older for the Chamber, 25 years for the Senate) and eligibility for election (25 years for the Chamber, 40 years for the Senate); the Constituent Assembly held that the greater maturity of senators would contribute to the reflective nature of the Senate;
c) the Senate may have a number of life senators; these are former Presidents of the Republic and five eminent individuals appointed by the President of the Republic for outstanding merit in the social, scientific, artistic and literary fields;

d) the Senate is more closely connected to the regions; to this end, the constitution envisages that senators are elected on a regional basis, each region having a minimum number of seven senators, with the exception of Molise which has two and Valle d'Aosta which has one.

Originally the two houses were designed to have different terms; five years for the Chamber and six for the Senate. This was a significant difference which was never actually applied since the first two Senates were dissolved prematurely at the same time as the Chamber (in 1953 and 1958) and, in 1963, Constitutional Law no. 2 was passed which unified the terms of the two houses.

As regards electoral laws, the Chamber was elected by proportional representation from party lists while the Senate was elected by the "first past the post" majority system. The Constituent Assembly redressed this difference with the electoral law of 1948, which stated that the Senate would be elected by the majority system only where the candidate in the constituency obtained 65% of the vote; failing this quorum, the seats would be distributed by the proportional system on a regional basis. As the threshold was extremely high, it was hardly ever reached and so, in practice, both houses were elected by proportional representation. Following the abrogative referendum of 1993, new electoral laws were passed (laws no. 276-277 1993) on the basis of which candidates in both houses run in single-member constituencies for ¾ of the seats and the remaining ¼ of seats are allocated by proportional representation. Some technical differences between the Chamber and the Senate remain, the most important is that the Senate is elected with a single ballot paper and the Chamber with two. In the last three legislatures, differences in the electorate and technical differences in the electoral system have resulted in two houses with slightly differing political configurations (the centre-left has always been slightly stronger in the Senate).

1. Parliament in joint session

Alongside the perfect bicameral system, the Constituent Assembly envisaged that both houses should meet as one to carry out certain functions; when this happens, parliament is said to be in joint session: this is a body composed of the Chamber and the Senate, and specifically a joint body which meets and debates autonomously in cases which are rigidly set out in the constitution.

These cases are:

- the election and the swearing in of the President of the Republic (when the President of the Republic is elected, the joint session of parliament is "supplemented" by three delegates for each region – Valle d'Aosta has one);

- the election of a third of the members of the Constitutional Court and the drafting, every nine years, of a list of 45 nominees, from which the aggregate judges of the Constitutional Court are chosen, in the case of penal judgement of the President of the Republic;
- the election of a third of the members of the Higher Council of the Judiciary (consiglio superiore della magistratura);
- the impeachment of the President of the Republic for high treason and offences against the constitution (judgement is referred to the Constitutional Court supplemented by 16 aggregate judges).

II. The Current Situation and Future Outlook for Bicameralism

1. Modifications to part II of the constitution

On 15 October 2004, the Chamber of Deputies passed an important bill, on its first reading, to amend the constitution. Bill AS2544-B is entitled "Reform to Part II of the Constitution", and should this reform go ahead, it would constitute the most significant amendment to the Basic Charter since 1948.

However, the law-making procedure for bill AS2544-B is still long and uncertain, especially if the so-called *navette* between the two houses is prolonged and if the proposal is passed with an absolute majority so that the opposition could challenge the reform by popular referendum. In accordance with Article 138 of the constitution, constitutional bills are passed only if the Chamber and Senate have voted favourably on the same text, twice consecutively, with an intervening period of three months. If, on a second reading, each house reaches a two thirds majority, the bill is passed immediately and published. If, however, the text is passed on a second reading with an absolute majority, a referendum may be called by a fifth of the members of the Chamber or by five hundred thousand voters or by five regional councils, within three months (as happened with the Constit. Law no. 3/2001, which went to referendum on October 7, 2001).

If a referendum is requested, the bill needs to receive the majority of valid votes to be passed. Unlike the abrogative referendum, which requires half plus one of those eligible to vote to cast their vote, there is no need for quorum to be reached.

Amongst the most innovative aspects of the constitutional reform bill is certainly the transformation of the Senate into a "Federal Senate", with differing responsibilities from the Chamber. The intention is to create a Chamber which represents the regions, keeping with the federalist transformation which has been in progress in Italy now for several years.

The construction of a federal system has been in progress in Italy in the last years. The first step towards a federal model was taken with the Constit. Law no. 1/1999, which introduced the direct election of the President of the Regions, with new and broader statutory powers for the ordinary regions. The second step was taken with Constit. Law no. 3/2001 (the so-called Reform of Title V). Rightly considered to be the most important constitutional law of the republican era, constitutional law no. 3 of 2001 has affected no fewer than 15 articles of the constitution, affecting more than 10% of its content.

The Reform of Title V has introduced substantial changes, notably the reversal of criteria for the allocation of responsibilities. The regions now hold legislative power in all matters, except for those specifically listed as exclusive and concurrent legislative powers of the state. However, the Reform of Title V is in itself incomplete, as expressed by the constitutional legislator. With clear reference to the creation of a future federal Senate, Article 11 of the Constitutional Law states that "until reform of Title I of the second part of the constitution" the rules of the Chamber and the Senate may envisage a supplementary parliamentary commission for regional questions, which include representatives of the local government (this is understood to be a surrogate for the Federal Chamber).

The third step towards a federal model of government is entrusted to the reform *in fieri*, which, amongst other things, should modify the Italian bicameral system, creating the much discussed Federal Senate.

2. *The transformation of the bicameral system and the construction of a federal senate*

While the Chamber of Deputies will only change structurally in number – going from six hundred and thirty to five hundred and eighteen members (eighteen of whom will be elected in overseas constituencies) – and eligible age – which will be reduced from 25 years to 21 – more far-reaching changes will affect the Senate. Senators will continue to be elected by direct universal suffrage on a regional basis. The Senate, however, will become a Federal Senate of the Republic and will undergo significant changes:

a) the number of elected Senators will be reduced from 315 to 252 and the overseas constituency will be eliminated: each Region will have at least 6 senators (except Molise and Valle d'Aosta);

b) voting age will be brought down from 25 years to 18, and eligibility from 40 years to 25;
c) life Senators will no longer exist; at their place will be introduced life Deputies;
d) the length of Senators' mandate will be subordinate to that of Regional Councils (the so called mechanism of contextuality) and so Senators will be elected together with their corresponding Regional Council and their mandate will terminate with the end of term of the Regional Assembly;
e) two representatives from each region will participate, without voting rights, in the activity of the Senate: one will be elected by the Regional Council and one by the Council of Local Government (the representative organ of local governing bodies within the regional system).

Point d) is of particular importance. Having the Senate elected and dissolved at the same time as the Regional Councils seems an interesting way to draw the Senate and the regions together. This scheme does not, however, satisfy the regions, who have called for a Senate based on the German *Bundesrat* model, a request which will probably be difficult to meet in the Italian context.

The project of constitutional reform envisages a clear separation of competences between the Chamber and the Senate, in the light of the differing attributions of authority to the state and the regions.

The modifications to Article 70 of the constitution concerning the legislative process are aimed to supersede perfect bicameralism, by virtue of which all legislative bills must be passed with identical texts by both houses of parliament.

According to the revised Article 70, the Chamber has the (exclusive) task to give confidence to the executive and to legislate on those matters exclusive to the state, as listed in the second paragraph of Article 117 (with some exceptions). It is the Senate's task to establish the fundamental principles (framework legislation) in matters of concurrent legislative powers, as indicated in the third paragraph of the same article. However, each House, on request, can propose amendments to the text passed by the other House (within thirty days); in this case the competent Chamber has the right to make the final decision on any proposed amendments.

In the case of framework legislation (passed by Senate), should the government believe that its amendments to a bill, having undergone examination in the Federal Senate, are essential for the implementation of government policy, or to safeguard its objectives, as in Article 120, second paragraph Constit., the President of the Republic can authorise the Prime Minister to explain his motivations to the Senate, which must make a decision within thirty days. If the Senate does not accept these amendments, the bill is sent to the Chamber which makes a final decision with an absolute majority of its members. This shift of powers in favour of the Chamber of Deputies is intended to safeguard the implementation of government policy. The Federal Senate, while freed of its fiduciary relationship, is however called upon to legislate in areas which may be of fundamental importance for government policy, and it was, therefore, natural to guarantee the prevalence of the political house.

Both houses are called upon to legislate on essential levels of services concerning civil and social rights; on electoral laws, governing bodies and fundamental functions of municipalities, provinces and metropolitan cities; on equalisation policies and fiscal federalism, as specified in Article 119 Constit.; on the substitutive powers of Article 120 Constit:; on the electoral system for the Chamber of Deputies and the federal Senate of the Republic; on cases where the constitution refers explicitly to the laws of the State or the laws of the Republic, specifically Articles 117, fifth and ninth paragraph, 118 second and fifth paragraph, 112, first paragraph, 125, 132, second paragraph, and 133 second paragraph. In cases where no agreement is reached between the two houses, their presidents can summon a committee composed of thirty Deputies and thirty Senators, charged with the task of drafting a unified text to submit to a final vote of the two assemblies. This is the so-called Mediating Committee, a body which already exists in other countries but not, as yet, in Italy.

To summarise, the text under examination introduces a three-part division of the legislative processes, as follows:

1. bills passed through the bicameral procedure;
2. bills of a unicameral nature with prevalence of the Chamber;
3. bills of a unicameral nature with prevalence of the Senate (but if the implementation of government policy is at stake, the Chamber prevails).

The result is a bicameral system with varying forms of powers.

The revised Article 70 is credited with overcoming the traditional difficulties inherent in the Italian legislative process (which is often at the mercy of the *navette* between the Chamber and the Senate), but it conceals an enormous problem: the definition of subject areas. It is a well-known fact that it is often difficult to know under which subject area a text falls. The final paragraph of Article 70 envisages that the presidents of the two houses will, by common accord, establish the criteria according to which a proposed bill may not contain dispositions relative to matters for which different processes should be applied, but it is difficult to say if this will be sufficient to overcome the obstacles.

3. The powers of parliament in joint session

There are important and far reaching innovations regarding joint sessions of parliament. Above all, the body called upon to elect the President of the Republic is no longer the Parliament in Joint Session supplemented with regional delegates, but the "Assembly of the Republic." According to the project, the Assembly of the Republic is a body composed of the components of the two houses, the presidents of the regional governments and the autonomous provinces of Trento and Bolzano and two delegates elected from each regional assembly (Valle d'Aosta has only one).

The Assembly of the Republic is present at the swearing in of the President of the Republic. At present, the President of the Republic is sworn in before Parliament in Joint Session, without those regional delegates who took part in the election procedure.

According to the project, joint sessions of parliament no longer have the power to elect members of the Higher Council of the Judiciary, nor members of the Constitutional Court (the election is attributed to the Chamber and the Senate respectively), nor the compilation of the list from which aggregate constitutional judges are chosen in trials against the President of the Republic (entrusted to the Chamber).

Parliament in Joint Session will retain however the power to impeach the President of the Republic for high treason or offences against the constitution.

Parliament in Joint Session should be newly empowered with the annulment of regional laws which are in contrast with the national interest. This existed previously (it was abolished by the reform of Title V), but was the preserve of the two houses rather than joint sessions of parliament. Under former Article 127 Constit., the government could bring questions in this regard before parliament, but as this power was never used, it was removed by the constitutional legislator.

II. FISCAL FEDERALISM

Hans W. Kopp

FISCAL FEDERALISM: SWITZERLAND

Introductory Note

Federalism has different historical roots, is differently structured and managed, has a different future in each country on the list for this workshop.

Still the common denominator always and invariably is the same: the recognition of the largest possible number of historical and other (normally traditional) differences in the political and legal culture underlying a free society on a given (normally national) territory as existing with acceptable reasons, and against this background the integration of all virtually destructive regional and local tendencies as constructive elements of a long-term democratic process.

My Introductory Note consists of the comments just made, plus an anecdote, plus the titles of three little chapters.

Here is the anecdote: A German, a French and a Swiss girl met in Basle and started quarrelling about how babies arrive on this earth. The German girl stated that the stork carries the children. The French girl replied: Nonsense! When mum and dad sleep together it takes roughly nine months and the baby is born. When they definitely could not agree they turned to the Swiss girl who so far had not contributed one single word and inquired: How is it with you? The Swiss girl prolonged her silence for another little moment and answered: With us this is different from one Canton to another.

And here are the titles of the three chapters I am going to suggest:

(I) Specific Essentials of Swiss Federalism

(II) Fiscal Federalism in the Confederation of Switzerland from 1848 to 2004

(III) Fiscal Federalism for Switzerland's Future.

I. Specific Essentials of Swiss Federalism

We exaggerate, but only to a small extent when we daresay that in Switzerland

- virtually all of the country's political wisdom has developed, and still develops from the bottom to the top, and not vice-versa;
- political experiences traditionally did grow from the Municipalities into the Cantons, and even more from the Cantons into the Confederation of Switzerland, and only exceptionally the other way around;
- to the traditional understanding of the typical Swiss citizen all funds mobilized and spent for public purposes always were, and still are generated within the Municipalities and the Cantons, and are so-to-speak "assigned" to a limited extent to the Confederation because in the long run there unfortunately is no other way to satisfactory solutions in the interest of all concerned.

Translated into the language of political biographies this means that virtually every Swiss politician, before he or she arrives at the top, is domesticated by tiresome years in the Municipalities and/or the Cantons. Typically he or she still is ambitious, but reasonably civilized towards the end of his or her way up from the grassroots. He or she is penetrated by the culture and civilization of intimate neighbourhood, of small groups, of mutual responsibilities rather than of power with all its virtual glamour and glory.

The Swiss girl quoted in the anecdote I shared with you some moments ago does not just make an amusing statement. She concentrates in a few simple words what must be called one of two mainstreams of Swiss political philosophy: In the symbolic language of our Federal Constitution the Swiss democracy as a whole consists of twenty-six "sovereign" democracies in which not far from everything is welcome to be "different from one Canton to another."

Werner Kägi, one of the recognized experts of Swiss constitutional law and practice in the 20th century, wrote in 1944: "The Confederation of Switzerland will either be governed by federalism, or no more exist." Georges-André Chevallaz, a prominent politician and less prominent historian, added in 1973: "In Switzerland federalism is more than an institution: it is fundamental for the country's existence"[1].

After dealing with these matters during several decades I would agree with both authors, and add that if a ranking of basic political values shall be required or at least permissible in the first line federalism and closely linked to it the autonomy of our almost 3,000 Municipalities have paved the way to Switzerland's functioning, stability, and overall political success.

1 Quoted from *Nüssli, K.*, Föderalismus in der Schweiz. Konzepte, Indikatoren, Daten. Zürcher Beiträge zur Politischen Wissenschaft Band 12 (Grüsch 1985) 11; translations by H.W.K.

Any day and hour and almost minute in Switzerland's political life is characterized by many – probably much too many – compromises. Federalism essentially is not a result of compromises. As surprising as this may sound to observers from abroad, comparing with federalism and municipal autonomy perhaps even democracy, and regrettably enough no doubt the rule of law system have been and are of secondary importance.

Whether we are pleased to state this or not the Confederation of Switzerland is one of the few classical variations of a federal system. In many respects our Confederation may be called a model democracy. However, I am sorry to reiterate that the Swiss Confederation is far from being a model state of law. In this respect we suffer from dramatic deficiencies which honestly to some extent are due to complications caused by federalism. It would be a wonderful goal for another workshop to provide an in-depth comparative analysis of conflicts of interest of this nature.

As the proof of the cake always is in the eating – no tongue should ever be used for talking about things which it has not tasted from very close –, I am going to insert three as I believe illustrative examples:

a) Traditionally, as all direct taxes always have been reserved for the Municipalities, and the Cantons above them, I pay no taxes on my income and capital to the federal authorities. Only in World War II, for financing military defense, the Confederation managed to obtain the competence to levy direct taxes. By virtue of provisions of federal constitutional law[2] such taxes still now are limited for certain periods of time (and therefore must periodically be approved again by cumulative majorities of the people and the Cantons), and also are limited as to maximum percentages to be applied. Apart from this "exception" direct taxes on income and capital are an exclusive domain of the Cantons and municipalities[3].

   Technically I still do not pay any tax on income and capital directly to "Berne" (the federal capital). Tax returns at least of all individuals are to be filed with the Municipalities, and are checked there, and in the Cantons; technically all moneys flow through the lower levels to the upper level.

   Subsidies made available by the Confederation to the Cantons often do reflect borderline situations. Equally often they are to be qualified as "political sins" which particularly after World War II have been committed more frequently than any spirit of federalism should have permitted.

---

2 Cf. Article 128 and (in the Chapter entitled "Transitory Provisions") Article 196 Clause 13 of the Swiss Federal Constitution of 18th April 1999.

3 Cf. in particular Article 128 Section 4 of the Swiss Federal Constitution of 1999.

b) I am a citizen of the Confederation of Switzerland, and the holder of a Swiss passport only and exclusively because I am a citizen of certain Municipalities and Cantons. Personally I am a citizen of Niederönz in the Canton of Berne because my ancestors have lived there for many generations, of the City of Lucerne in the Canton of Lucerne because my grandparents and parents earned their living and were active as militia politicians in that City, and I am a citizen of Zumikon in the Canton of Zurich because my own family has had its domicile there for forty years. My wife has two more citizenships: the one of the City of St. Gall in the Canton of St. Gall because her family was happy there for more than a century, and the one of Unterbäch in the Canton of Valais because it was granted to her by the local inhabitants as a token of honour and gratitude.

c) When a number of years ago the Swiss Federal Minister of Defense landed on an alp in the Canton of Grisons with a fleet of helicopters and a bunch of generals and colonels around him who were more numerous than the sheeps and goats running away he immediately wanted to start a discussion about the implications of utilizing the alp as a shooting range and training ground. He had hardly said two words when he was briskly interrupted by the president of the local municipality who had walked up there on his own feet and exclaimed: Sorry, Sir, this is my territory. I absolutely insist on my privilege to welcome you and your guests in the name of my Municipality before you open any meeting up here. The federal minister did shut his mouth, listened to the very warm greetings which were in fact offered to him, and then switched to the order of the day.

At this point, Ladies and Gentlemen, I have got to warn you. So far we have tried to be pragmatic, and as colourful and entertaining as our three girls might be after at least three suitable boys from some further nations would have joined them. From now on this presentation will be systematic without any compromise, and therefore dry and boring to death.

Honestly: what are the leading guidelines of Swiss federalism?

We will insist on an extensive interpretation and application of the principle of subsidiarity, on a creative equality among all member states, and on an equally creative separation of powers embedded in a network of power splitting:

(1) Everybody knows what subsidiarity means: that whatever can reasonably be decided or left open or done or not done at the lowest possible level shall not be taken care of at any higher level.

At first sight such a statement may look clear and convincing, but neither in theory nor in practice it will provide us with satisfactory tools. As with regard to the principle of federalism, and to most other and further principles of public life the devil always is in the detail.

In particular the question will be of the essence who shall be competent to decide what reasonably can be mastered at the lower level. To our mind it would be a misunderstanding of the idea of subsidiarity to leave such determination to the exclusive discretion of any higher-ranking authority. In all cases of doubt the opposite shall be true: that the political bodies at the lower level shall be entitled and also enabled to make their choice, and will not be disturbed in solving their problems themselves. Over and above this there must be a permanent exchange of opinions among the lower level bodies on the one side, and between them and the respective higher level bodies on the guidelines and borderlines of higher level interventions on the other side. Nothing will be dictated from the higher level without the lower level bodies jointly and severally having at least had a fair chance to make themselves heard.

We are tempted to suggest a term like overall subsidiarity for referring to a further aspect of Swiss federalism: According to its underlying philosophy the relationship between the Confederation and the Cantons which usually dominates the discussion shall be embedded in a much farther-reaching realm of subsidiarities. What is adequate between the Confederation and the Cantons shall as a matter of principle also be adequate between the Cantons and the Municipalities, and ultimately between the Municipalities and all individual citizens and inhabitants and any smaller or bigger group or organisation they have got to tolerate and support. It would be fascinating, but of course is impossible to develop in the framework of this presentation the applicability and limits of subsidiarity between the Confederation and the Municipalities and groups and individuals, and between each Canton and all groups and individuals.

(2) The second specific characteristic of federalism in Switzerland is creative equality. We are going to concentrate now exclusively on the relationship between the Confederation and the Cantons. Within this relationship, and analogies would of course again apply beyond its limits, the goal never has been just to respect a strictly formal equality among all Cantons. The idea always has been that there must be active interventions proving solidarity from the top as well as mutually among all Cantons. The Swiss Confederation essentially dates back to 1291. In its first historical periods not even a common governing body was deemed to be necessary. The alliance was

just one of mutual help and assistance[4]. It may sound strange, but somehow this original spirit has survived over many centuries. Equality without creative elements facilitating to even the smallest mountain Canton to participate as a full partner in its own right, far beyond its relative demographic or economic strength, and to contribute to the joint pursuit of happiness would be considered quite hypocritical.

(3) What do we mean, thirdly, with a creative overall separation of powers? So far I have not been able to trace any other political system than the one of Switzerland in which the classical separation of powers was extended and re-interpreted so intensively into other and further areas of applicability. Federalism and the autonomy of Municipalities in this optics are the result of a highly and specifically developed separation of powers as to territory. In Switzerland we do rather exaggerate as to the separation of powers in time: Even all judges are subject to political re-election every few yeas which is dangerous for a high-quality judicial system. We have learned from the old Romans that nobody shall chair high political bodies for normally more than one year. For example there is no president or chairperson of an executive branch of any federal or cantonal government who would not mandatorily be replaced after about twelve months. Federalism fits perfectly well into the widespread distrust again any consolidation, concentration, prolongation of powers.

II. Fiscal Federalism in the Confederation of Switzerland from 1848 to 2004

1848 is the year in which the present Confederation of Switzerland was established. If it shall at all be possible to summarize what happened between 1848 and the end of this current year 2004 this implicity means that a lot may have occurred, but not much must be outlined in the framework of our Workshop of these very days[5].

---

4 *de Rougemont, D.*, Die Schweiz. Modell Europas (Wien/München, original edition in the French language Paris 1965) 67: According to *de Rougemont* federalism as a clearly defined political goal is a relatively modern phenomenon which dates back only to the first third of the 20th century. However, its roots are quite old. The original Swiss Federal Treaty of 1291 did provide neither for a common authority, nor for joint policies, with the only exception of the duty and obligation to mutual assistance among the Cantons.

5 For a short, but very conclusive summary see *Hafner F.*, Die neue Bundesverfassung im Kontext der Verfassungen, Entwürfe und Reformversuche seit 1798, in: Zeit-

The exact birthday of the first Federal Constitution of the Confederation of Switzerland is 12th September, 1848. It is often forgotten nowadays that based on older traditions votes of the people were considered severally in each individual Canton, but never formally added up for a nationwide comparison, and that against this background the first Federal Constitution was deemed approved by a majority of 15.5 Cantons only. In the final Assembly of the Cantons one further Canton joined the majority which led to the result for the history books of 16.5 against 5.5 Cantons. Between 1848 and the end of 2004 there have been two total revisions of our Federal Constitution: one on 29th May 1874, and one on 18th April, 1999. There also have been numerous partial revisions which as the total revisions require the cumulative majorities of the people and of the Cantons.

It was of course not by chance that in the year 1959 an important Federal Law on Financial Equalization among the Cantons was adopted. This Law still is in force now, and will probably be valid and applicable until 31st December, 2007. World Wars I and II and the political and economic crisis in Europe of the Thirties and Fourties had changed a lot in our country as well, equality among the Cantons was endangered, important social burdens had become too heavy for many of them, against Switzerland's best traditions centralization had been accelerated.

On Sunday, 28th November, 2004, i.e. just a few days ago an all-embracing Reform Legislation has been adopted by a majority of 64.4% against 35.6% by the people, and simultaneously by a majority of 20.5 against 2.5 Cantons, or of 89.1% against 10.9% of the Cantons. The usual English abbreviation for the new Law is RET (Reform of Financial Equalization and Task Allocation between the Confederation and the Cantons), the German abbreviation NFA (Neugestaltung des Finanzausgleichs und der Aufgabenteilung zwischen Bund und Kantonen), the French abbreviation RPT (Réforme de la péréquation financière et de la repartition des tâches entre la Confédération et les cantons), the Italian abbreviation NPC (Nuova impostazione della perequazione finanziaria e della ripartizione dei compiti tra Confederazione e Cantoni). The RET comprises amendments of 27 Articles of the Swiss Federal Constitution of 1999, and more than thirty projects at the level of statutory law. If all works out according to the timing agreed upon the RET shall become legally effective as from 1st January, 2008.

---

schrift für Schweizerisches Recht (ZSR) / Revue de droit suisse / Rivista di diritto svizzero / Revista da dretg svizzer Neue Folge 120 (2001) 1. Halbband 11 et sqq., with an excellent summary on Pages 41/42.

Actually, what went wrong, in other words why was the necessity of RET recognized by the Executive Branch of our Federal Government, chronologically parallel to this in most of the mass-media and by most of the political parties, subsequently by both Chambers of our National Parliament (one representing the people, and the other one representing the Cantons), finally by large majorities of the people and the Cantons?

There has been a situation not far from a national consensus that in five essential directions our political system, as far as federalism is concerned, had to be revitalized. There is somewhat less agreement on how the future of federalism shall look. On one side of the political arena prominent groups appeared to be afraid that creative equality among the Cantons might go too far, and thus prejudice the country's capabilities to survive and compete. On the opposite side of the arena we observe tendencies to give a high priority to federalism, but even a higher one to social measures, in particular to subsidies of any description. Particularly one Canton, the one of Zoug, was afraid that within the framework of equalization financial burdens to be carried by itself might be too heavy. Organizations of, and in favour of disabled persons arranged for quite emotional public demonstrations because in the future primarily the Cantons will be responsible for assisting them, and they were afraid that this will be disadvantageous for them.

Now, these are the five essential directions in which according to wide-spread opinions federalism has got to be revitalized:

(1) In the past, particularly after World War II the Confederation as well as the Cantons and Municipalities politically speaking were active, often probably overactive. At the beginning there had been rather elementary, but quite clear concepts how to intervene, and when and why not to intervene, but in the permanent confrontation with the complex problems of a rapidly developing modern society original concepts were soon obsolete. What had to be done was mostly done, and often done too generously, but often late, often with vague goals, often depending upon where and how funds could relatively easily and quickly be made available. The result was a jungle of parallel or conflicting duties and competences of authorities satisfactorily cooperating and negotiating with each others, of politicians talking at cross-purposes, of overlapping activities, of more instruments than purposes, of funds not producing best possible results.

(2) As often only the Confederation was strong enough to cope with new or bigger requirements Cantons were more and more moved into a defensive position. Federalism as the fathers of our Federal Constitution had understood it was downgraded to regional autonomy (comparable to the local

autonomy of Municipalities). The ugly reference to an "executive federalism", i.e. to a degenerated federalism serving for a reliable execution of the Confederation's orders, came up. Such developments weakened the traditionally rather smooth, at any rate very close relationships between the Cantons on the one side, and Municipalities and individuals on the other side, and damaged political and moral solidarity at all levels. Cantons and Municipalities often were willing to act, but were not aware and could not find out quickly and reliably enough how far they could and should go, particularly because earlier or later there might be federal interventions anyhow.

(3) The Confederation more and more was overloaded with tasks and responsibilities, and could not satisfactorily focus on the issues which exclusively, or at least primarily were to be taken care by itself.

(4) Criteria for federal assistance and interventions were not sufficiently logical and transparent, or simply wrong. For example Cantons could under many circumstances make available federal subsidies just by choosing expensive solutions or otherwise spending more, instead of having to prove that and why their own resources were not strong enough. By the same token it became the specific knowledge of professional experts in the various administrations involved when and where and how the maximum could be obtained out of the federal treasury. This kind of a peculiar "secret science" was nothing for militia politicians who normally changed positions anyhow after a few years.

Bureaucracy was unduly strengthened against the executive branches of the national and cantonal governments, and also against parliaments at all levels.

(5) As virtually all political solutions were dictated by opportunism, at least by an overdosis of pragmatism cooperation among the Cantons was seriously damaged. Another reason for the same development was that differences among the Cantons were becoming too big. Cantonal egoisms prevailed where traditionally solidarity should have been demonstrated. The usual pretention was that sooner or later the Confederation would have to become active anyhow. Why should a stronger or specifically "richer" Canton sacrify a lot as due to the lack of recognized clear-cut criteria nobody might even note it, except perhaps the inhabitants of the "giving Canton" who would start shouting and crying when their tax burdens continued growing or could not be diminished not even because of themselves, but in the sole interest of their neighbours?

First studies on how that labyrinthic jungle could be re-converted into an orderly Swiss forest were initiated in the early Nineties. In 1994 the RET Project was officially started. Twice, in 1996 and 1999, all Cantons and political groups and large selections of further political tendencies of almost any description were confronted with essential projects and proposals, and invited to file their objections and opinions. Subsequently the so-called Messages to both Chambers of the Federal Parliament were drafted and presented by the Executive Branch of the Federal Government. During all these phases numerous public hearings were held, and experts' opinions obtained. The RET is considered as a federal project, but from the very beginning all Cantons have been directly and actively involved. The Conference of Cantonal Governments had nominated their own RET Spokesman, and had delegated one further representative into the Top Project Management of the Confederation. Such representative, however, was and is paid by the Cantons. The full texts not only of the amendments of the Federal Constitution, but also of essentially all adjustments required at the level of statutory law were made known to the public before the final campaign which now has ended on 28th November, 2004 even began. In the event that unexpected hardships would result from the RET Project against any Canton such effects will be mitigated by virtue of specific mechanisms which will be valid, with degressive effects, for 28 full years, i.e. from 1st January, 2008 when the RET shall become effective until 31st December, 2035 (our dear European Union friends will gather from this information that we will hardly be able to join them before 2036 as the opposite might cause some little disadvantage to one of our small mountain Cantons).

III. Fiscal Federalism for Switzerland's Future

With regard to federalism there are parallel truths as with regard to parliamentarism. In the long run parliaments are unable to maintain their political strength without strong financial powers. The same applies, *mutatis mutandis*, on member states. However, neither for parliaments nor for member states financial powers are the only test of health and survival. If financial powers are not embedded in a suitable political and legal environment experiences will show that economic influence and competence alone cannot suffice. Fiscal, financial, economic powers are like a strong motor. The strongest motor, though, will not guarantee a safe arrival if the boat is a misconstruction, or the sea too rough.

If at this point I may suddenly switch back from one metaphor to the other, i.e. from motor-boats back to the jungle, Switzerland must cut down and burn many plants before being able to see through again, and to bring up fresh young trees. The watchword in this respect is to disentangle (in German: zu *entflechten*, zu *entwirren*; en français *débrouiller*; in italiano *strigare* o *sbrogliare*; en español *desendredar*, o *desenmarañar*). Dozens of specific measures taken in the past whenever it was deemed appropriate had to be analyzed, and to be substituted by a small number of systematically developed versatile instruments.

Implicitly we already have stated that with regard to the RET Project the Confederation never along the way claimed what in German we would call a "Kompetenz-Kompetenz", i.e. a constitutional power to define unilaterally the powers of the Cantons, and also of the Municipalities. The RET Project thus became a public joint venture of the Confederation of Switzerland and its member states.

From here on everything was simple and logical as far as anything in politics can be simple and logical.

Rights and responsibilities could be split up among four different addressees: first of all, each Canton severally; secondly, all or part of the Cantons jointly, presupposing that they will agree among themselves what is to be accomplished by whom; thirdly, the Confederation in a joint venture with all or part of the Cantons; and fourthly, last but not least, the Confederation alone.

In pursuance of the principle of subsidiarity whatever can be achieved by the addressees one, two, three shall be achieved by them, and only what reasonably is not feasible at the lower or combined levels shall be left to the Confederation.

Decisions are to be made as closely as possible to the individual citizens. Those who decide must bear the financial consequences of their decisions.

All public bodies ultimately must get their accounts approved by the parliaments, and in many instances directly by the people.

We realize, of course, that we make ourselves unable to get identical public goods and services delivered everywhere in our country. We prefer equivalent goods and services to be shaped according to regional and local requirements (or as the case may be, predilections). Even in the event that institutions and procedures could be perfect, as they will never be, federalism only can survive in a climate of mutual tolerance.

We often are asked whether minority protection is the main goal of federalism. It certainly is not. However, a well-functioning federal system will normally provide an efficient form of protection of most or all minorities.

In brackets we may insert here that on 28th November, simultaneously with the RET, or in German NFA (Neuer Finanzausgleich) the NFO (Neue Finanzordnung) was adopted by even larger majorities, more precisely by 73.8% of the people and astonishing 95.7% of the Cantons. The Confederation of Switzerland would have had no more competence to levy direct taxes on capital and income, as well as the VAT, after 31st December 2006.[6] In 2003 such taxes were the equivalent of about 63%, or almost two-thirds, of the total federal revenues. Direct taxes and VAT have been prolonged now until 31st December 2020 (the longest prolongation ever granted to the Confederation), but maximum tax rates still are limited by virtue of the Federal Constitution, and therefore may only be adjusted by cumulative majorities of the people and the Cantons.

At present about one-third of all public moneys are spent by the Cantons, a few per cent more than one-third by the Confederation, a few per cent less than one-third by the Municipalities.

Financial and fiscal differences among the Cantons are legally and factually accepted, but they have become too big. Proportions in the order of magnitude of 5 : 2 between the total public expenditure per capita of cantonal and municipal governments in two specific Cantons, or also of 5 : 2 as to total tax burdens are exceptional, but do occur.

Our political system aims at causing the Cantons and Municipalities to compete with each others. The official philosophy is that the more ardently they do compete the more efficiently they will be managed, and the more attractive they can in the overall become for taxpayers. One of the main targets of RET is to encourage political units to show stronger ambitions, and to make the country as a whole more competitive.

It obviously is wrong that exclusively due to his bigger ambitions or disrespect or negligence the one who spends more may be able to obtain higher subsidies from the Confederation. The index of financial strength used so far which has often caused or at least permitted an unsatisfactory channelling of public moneys is superseded. A resource indicator directly based on the resource potential of each Canton will take its place. The average resource indicator of all Cantons is set to 100 points. Cantons with a resource indicator of more than

6 Article 196 Clauses 13 and 14 Section 4 of the Swiss Federal Constitution of 18th April 1999.

100 points are deemed to be financially strong, the others are considered as financially weak. The new rather sophisticated resource equalization will lift them to at least 85 points. Resource equalization will be financed by the richer Cantons, and only as far as the burden would become unduly heavy for them by the Confederation. When RET becomes effective on 1st January 2008 six Cantons or "Half-Cantons" will probably have to pay in favour of the other twenty.[7]

Resource equalization will be supplemented by a system of burden equalization, or if you prefer cost compensation among the Cantons. On the one side geographic and topographic criteria will help the Cantons in the mountainous areas, on the other side the so-called socio-demographic criteria will be in favour of the big agglomerations with their heavy welfare and infrastructure burdens.

The fact that dozens of tasks are disentangled, and regrouped in big clearly defined parcels should make an efficient controlling much easier.

For paving the way to your as I hope quite critical questions and comments I now suggest to reiterate very briefly part of what has been outlined, labelling paragraphs with degressive numbers from thirty down to one:

- As a consequence of the RET more than 30 statutory laws will be adjusted, or added to the existing federal laws.
- 27 Articles of the Federal Constitution have been amended.
- 11 tasks will in the future be the exclusive domain of the Cantons (examples: certain areas of public education, financial contributions below the university level, homes and workshops for disabled persons).
- 9 tasks are earmarked for future intercantonal cooperation (examples: universities, medium-level vocational schools, top medicine).
- 7 tasks are exclusively reserved to the Confederation (examples: national defense, national throughways, old age insurance).
- 5 pillars will be specifically developed:
    - the disentanglement of burdens and costs:
    - resource equalization;

---

7 Switzerland consists of 23 Cantons three of which are divided into two Half-Cantons each. The distinction between Cantons and Half-Cantons to a large extent is of historical interest only. Two important differences nowadays are that in the "Senate" of the Confederation (House of the Cantons) Half-Cantons are entitled to only one seat instead of two, and that in national referendums as far as majorities of the Cantons are required Half-Cantons have only half of the weight of a "normal" Canton.

- equalization of burdens to be borne by the Cantons;
- cooperation Confederation / Cantons;
- cooperation among Cantons, to a large extent in pursuance of new rules and regulations.

- 4 public domains are to be systematically distinguished: the ones of individual Cantons, of joint ventures among Cantons, of joint ventures Confederation/Cantons, of the Swiss Confederation as such.
- In 3 specific equalization areas assistance will be provided to Cantons fulfilling specific requirements: resource equalization, geographic and topographic cost compensation, socio-demographic cost compensation.
- In 2 directions competition among the Cantons will be enhanced: performance as to the production and delivery of public goods and services, fiscal attractivity.
- All efforts are directed towards 1 main goal: the efficient revitalization, and to a large extent re-invention of Swiss federalism[8].

---

8 Acknowledgments: The author is most grateful to the Top Management Staff of RET for the information and materials generously provided. Cooperation with them has been a real source of pleasure and satisfaction, and illustrated the exceptional quality of the contributions made by the Staff to all authorities involved. Two Gentlemen deserve to be specifically mentioned: *Mr. Fred Bangerter* of the Swiss Federal Administration, and *Dr. oec. Walter Moser*, representative of the Conference of Cantonal Governments in the Top Management Staff nominated by the Executive Branch of the Federal Government.

PETER BUßJÄGER

REFORMS ON FISCAL FEDERALISM IN AUSTRIA

I. Principles of Federal Fiscal Relations between Federal Level, Länder and Municipalities

1. Principles of the fiscal constitution

In Austria, federal fiscal relations are not outlined in the federal constitution of 1920 itself, but in a special Fiscal Constitution Act of 1948 (F-VG) and in a special "Law of Financial Equalisation", which means in fact a so-called "Tax Sharing Law", which operates only for a limited period (in the past for four years).

The financial constitution system is very clearly shaped according to the decentralization theory of federalism. States and communities are treated as "lower territorial units" that, in a strict sense, are only different versions of local government at numerous levels and with various competencies.[1]

The power to assign and share taxes is not reserved to constitutional law, but is left to ordinary federal legislation. Federal law must assign taxes within an abstract constitutional framework of various types of shared or exclusive tax allocation. The most important types are:

- Exclusive federal taxes
- Taxes divided between federal level and municipalities
- Exclusive state taxes
- Exclusive local (municipalities) taxes.

The Länder are free to "invent" new taxes as long as they do not concurrent with federal laws concerning taxes. In practice, these so-called "taxation autonomy" of the Länder has no importance.

---

1 *Pernthaler*, Austrian Federalism, in: *Rose/Traut* (eds.), Federalism and Decentralization (2001), p. 132.

2. *Principles of financial equalisation (tax sharing) between federal government, Länder and local level*

The "Law of Financial Equalisation" (FAG) is acted by the federal parliament with its both chambers, the National Council und and the Federal Council on ground of the Financial Constitution (F-VG). The basic principles of the F-VG state that each government must bear the costs of its own activities (sec. 2) and that all provisions regarding taxing powers and tax sharing must enable the different levels of government to finance their tasks with revenues from their own sources (sec. 4).

It is remarkable that the second chamber of the Austrian federal parliament, the federal council, has in these essential matters for the Länder only a suspensive veto.[2]

As it was said above, the law of financial equalisation is usually acted for a limited period, formerly for six years (up to 1985), now usually three to four years.[3] A new act was adopted by the federal parliament to the end of 2004 and will be valid until 2008.

The main part of revenue of all levels is generated within the so-called joint (shared) taxation system. This complex tax sharing forms the basis with some special sources aside (own taxes, grants, fees and charges, public debt).

The sharing itself is carried out in a complicated manner. In a first step (so-called "Oberverteilung"), the total revenue of a single tax is divided between the Bund, Länder and municipalities according to the ratios negotiated for the different taxes. In a second step (so-called "Unterverteilung") the total shares for Länder and municipalities are divided between the nine Länder and then the total share for the municipalities per state is divided among its municipalities.

In practice tripartite negotiations take place between the three levels of Austria's political system (federal level, Länder and municipalities) before the adoption of such a new law leading to political agreements about tax-sharing for the given period. These negotiations result in a compromise agreement on "financial equalisation", its ratios and criteria for division, and some vertical grants to and from a level with important horizontal equalising effects.[4] Though these negotiations may be seen as an example of the Austrian "social

---

2 Art. 42 Federal Constitution (B-VG).

3 See also *Thöni*, Fiscal Federalism in Austria: facts and new developments, in: *Fossati/Panella* (eds.), Fiscal Federalism in the European Union (1999), p. 110.

4 *Thöni*, Fiscal Federalism, p. 110.

partnership"[5] the bargaining positions of the federal government and the "lower" governments are in respect of the legal framework very unequal. States and local governments really have no legal alternative but to accept the determination of fiscal relations by the federal government.

Although the legal position of the Länder (and the local governments) is weak, it is their political power in connection with their competence to execute federal administration, which compensates this unsatisfying position in some aspects.[6] In addition, the Austrian Constitutional Court rules that the compromise agreement between the federal government, states and municipalities indicates that the financial adjustment law is justified. In the case that such an settlement is not existing, the court would have to decide, if the law of the financial equalisation is appropriate and justified.[7]

3. *Intergovernmental relations in financial matters*

In addition to this system of financial relations there are two concordats between the federal government, the Länder and the municipalities, which should be explicitly mentioned in this context: Namely the Concordat on a consultation mechanism[8] and the Concordat on an Austrian Stability Pact.[9] Both concordats were not just concluded by the federation and the Länder, but also by the municipalities (represented by the Austrian Association of Towns and the Austrian Association of Municipalities). According to Art. 15a of the federal constitution (B-VG) whereafter only the federation and the Länder are permitted to conclude such concordats, this would not have been possible. A Constitutional Act of Authorization had therefore to be passed in order to empower the municipalities to take part in these two concordats. This new type of parity, which includes the municipalities as well, allows some discussion on a possible development towards a "three-layered-federalism." Since the classical concept of federalism does not recognize municipalities as constituent parts of the federal state and as long as this new dimension is not lim-

5 *Thöni*, Fiscal Federalism, p. 110.

6 See also *Thöni*, Fiscal Federalism, p. 108.

7 See for example the judgement of the Constitutional Court from March 13th, 2003, G 248/02.

8 BGBl. I Nr. 35/1999.

9 Presently valid: Österreichischer Stabilitätspakt 2001, BGBl. I Nr. 39/2002. A new Stability Pact between the Bund, the Länder and representatives of the cities and municipalities was signed in November 2004 and will be approved by the parliaments during the first month of 2005.

ited to the question of financial equality, however, local government is still not an integral element of the federal system as a whole.

The consultation mechanism obliges the Bund and Länder to consult each other and the municipalities if a draft law or an ordinance of one entity would impose financial burdens on the others. In this case, the matter is discussed by the consultation committee which consists of representatives of all three territorial levels. If the committee fails to reach an agreement on the matter, the entity that intends to pass the law will be responsible for any additional costs. This mechanism protects the Länder from federal laws that would have a financial impact on them; on the other hand, the Länder themselves will run the risk of bearing additional costs if they enact laws against the will of the others.

The concordat of the Austrian Stability Pact 2001 was concluded under the rigorous pressure of the EU convergence criteria. According to this pact the Länder must achieve an annual budgetary surplus, whereas, to a certain extent, a deficit is possible on part of the federation and at least a balanced budget on part or the municipalities. This means to force the Länder into this concordat was a provision in the recent Tax Equalisation Act, which threatened them with considerable financial sanctions if they refused to sign the concordat. This example clearly shows that political and also legal force may be used even in that is called "cooperative federalism", although it hast to be admitted that his was the most outstanding case of its kind.[10] Now the partners of the Austrian Stability Pact 2001 have concluded a new settlement for the period from 2005-2008, without any substantial change.[11]

It might be seen as paradox, but in a whole the two mentioned concordats have strengthened not only cooperative federalism in Austria, but also the Länder and – primarily – the municipalities. These entities are recognized not only as essential parts of the federal systems – this is primarily a result of the constitutional framework. It is their role as partners of the federal government, which is remarkable.

4. Analysis

An analysis of the states' position in Austria's financial system leads to the following conclusions:

- The states have no major taxes of their own.[12]

---

10 See also *Gamper*, Legislative and executive Gonvernance in Austria (2004), p. 21.

11 See also below under 4.

12 There are some own taxes of the Länder but without essential relevance.

- Their main revenues come from sharing joint federal taxes in a tripartite system, together with local governments, their shares fixed by federal law.
- A substantial part of their revenues is derived from transfers of other governments, thereby increasing the dependency of states and local governments.
- There is a substantial reverse flow of state and local community funds to the federal government by means of unofficial financial settlements. This "gray financial settlement" is regulated by private legal agreements and instruments or by political "gentlemen's agreements" between governments.

The effect of these four elements is that the Austrian states are nearly completely dependent upon the federal government as far as their finances are concerned. On the other side stands their role as partners of the federal government in the concordats and in the negotiations in financial equalisation.

Taxing in Austria is, on the one hand, very coordinated because of strong centralisation and a strong tax-sharing system. On the other hand, fiscal equivalence to interlock "beneficiaries", "payers" and "deciders" gets lost. Tax-sharing systems have a great advantage that they provide means to harmonise local und regional revenue differences and reduce risks of economic fluctuation and their influence upon tax revenues. On the other hand, a tax-sharing system such as in Austria inevitably reduces the independence and autonomy of individual governments and governments' levels, usually strengthening the higher level.[13]

Spending and financing responsibilities in several areas are mixed between the federal government and the Länder or between various authorities. Examples are, inter alia, the provision of means-tested income replacement benefits for the unemployed, the funding of teachers and the financing of waste water purification facilities and networks. This can cause significant inefficiency in resource allocation, making fiscal consolidation policies more difficult and reducing policy effectiveness in areas such as labour market of educational reform.[14]

Therefore reforms of the Austrian Financial Constitution should envisage the closing of some gaps between "beneficiary", "payer" und "decider", reminding that some own taxation is fundamental for federal systems.[15]

---

13 *Thöni*, Fiscal Federalism, p. 116 f.

14 See also OECD Economic Survey – Austria 2003 (www.oecd.org/document 36/).

15 See also *Thöni*, Fiscal Federalism, p. 117.

II. The Project "Austrian Convention" – General Remarks

The current Austrian Constitution was mostly drawn up by the jurisprudent Hans Kelsen in 1920. In its version of 1929, it is still valid today. However, the Austrian constitution has been changed more than 80 times. Today, it consists of more than 1,000 constitutional provisions and is thus somewhat confusing.

Debates on reforming Austria's constitution have a long tradition. The Austrian federal constitution is not codified in one single "constitutional act" but consists in a great number of old and new constitutional statutes and provisions. In addition, the federal system is very centralized and its efficiency is doubtful, the fundamental rights need to be codified in one single charta. In the past, many commissions failed to create a new, modern federal system or a new charta for fundamental rights.

On 30 June 2003, the Austrian Convention started to work with its first, inaugural meeting in Vienna's Parliament. Subsequently ten working groups were formed.

The Convention's tasks were to work out proposals for reforming the Austrian state and constitution. Therefore, the Austrian Convention was also called 'Constitutional Convention' by the public. With the future constitution, the Austrian state should be able to fulfil its tasks in a cost-effective, transparent and citizen-friendly way.

The convention had established ten committees, which had to discuss different themes of the reforming project. Until the end of 2004, the members of the Convention as divided into the ten working groups had to go through the constitution, to define the relation between federal government, provincial diets and the European Union, and to work out responsibilities. One of these themes were questions of the financial constitution, which had to be discussed In committee 10.

The convention finished its work in Januray 2005 without reaching consent in the most intensively debated matters such as the division of competencies, restructuring financial relationships between federal level, Länder and municipalities or creating a new charta of fundamental rights including social guarantees.

III. Dealing with Financial Matters within the Austria Convention

The presidency of the Austrian Convention had given the committee a mandate to make proposals to the following theme[16]:

> "Reform of the financial constitution, especially under the point of view of the combination of income and expense control and of a revenue equalization based on the requirements."

Committee 10 hat finished its work in December 2004. The reason for the late finalisation was that committee 10 was also the last of the working groups of the Austrian Convention, which started with its work. The working group submitted in July 2004 one first report, which showed pretty few consent in essential questions, such as in respect of taxation autonomy of the Länder or bringing together spending and financing responsibilities.[17]

Also presently, after finalisation of the convention, it does not seem that the consent has grown.[18] As regards instruments of fiscal federalism there are no results, which would be worth to be mentioned.

Therefore we cannot expect any essential change of the current system of financial relations between federal government, Länder and municipalities. The crucial provision of the Austrian financial constitution, whereafter the federal level decides, if the Länder and municipalities should be empowered to raise taxes, will not be touched.

This is because not only the federal government but even more the Länder are not interested in any responsibility for raising taxes. There were only discussions, if the Länder should be empowered to raise some taxes such as taxes on real estates. Not even in this point the committee could reach any consent. Though one could critizise the very restrictive attitude of the Austrian Länder towards raising taxes by own, their argument that it would not make sense, to have competences only in respect of some few some taxes, which have no important income, seems to be reasonable in principle.[19]

On the other hand the Länder and the municipalities proposed that the three levels of government in Austria should have guaranteed for a longer period certain shares of the whole tax income of the state. In the opinion of the Länder such a guaranteed share would lead to more transparency and to more

---

16 See also www.konvent.gv.at.

17 Report of working group 10 from July 15th, 2004.

18 See report of working group 10 from November 30th, 2004.

19 See the discussion within working group 10 (report from July 15th, 2004, p. 22).

responsibility for spending money on all levels of the state. This proposal, however, did not find the support of the federal government.[20]

There are various reasons for this negative attitude towards fiscal federalism: First, there is the fear that competition in raising taxes will lead to a destroying competition between the Länder and will be a problem for disadvantaged areas in the east and the south of Austria. Secondly, lobbies representing economic interests opposed to fiscal federalism and thirdly, living the ideas of federalism is in Austria underdeveloped.

Summarizing, we have to state that we cannot expect any essential change of the present system of division of competences in fiscal federalism. So the system will stay the same: With a wide-ranged tax raising power of the federal government, which will leave no more space for fiscal federalism in Austria. Worse, there is not any interest on the side of the Länder that this system should be changed.

This leads to the question, how the new "act for financial equalisation" will deal with the need of Länder and municipalities for financial support.

IV. The New "Law of Financial Equalisation" for 2005-2008: No Step towards Fiscal Federalism

In November of 2004, after long debates an agreement between the federal minister for finances, the nine governors of the Länder (Landeshauptmänner) and the representatives of the cities and municipalities was concluded, in which the principles of the next Law of Financial Equalisation between the federal level, the Länder and the Cities and Municipalities were fixed.

Even though the act of legislation had not yet passed the parliament at this date, it was sure that – after closing the agreement – the financial equalisation between the three levels of government in Austria is for the next four years definite. In the meantime the new act was set into force.[21]

During the past negotiations, the federal minister for finances tried to impose some aspects of the fiscal federalism in Austria's financial system. Finally he failed – for the same reasons as it was in case of the debates in working group 10 of the Austrian Convention: The Länder were not interested to raise some selected taxes, as for example the tax on real estates.

---

20 See report of working group 10 from July 15th, 2004, p. 21 ff.

21 BGBl. I Nr. 156/2004.

The new financial equalisation brought only few modifications in comparison with the last one. It is, however, remarkable that the tendency of the past, to reduce the shares of Länder and municipalities in favour of the federal government could be stopped. The Bund will get about 73.2% of the whole income of the state, the Länder 15.2% and the municipalities 11.6%. This also shows the enormous grade of centralization within the Austrian system.

In the context of the discussions about the new financial equalisation the three levels of government also reached consent about the principles of the new Stability Pact for the period 2005-2008: The Bund will be allowed to make a deficit 2.3% of the BIP in 2005, the Länder should achieve a surplus of 0.6% of the BIP und and the municipalities may have in common equalised budgets.

So we can state that also the new act for financial equalisation will bring no further step towards fiscal federalism, with one single exception: The Länder will be empowered to raise a contribution from persons, who need the services of a hospital. These contributions will reach the amount of 15 Mio Euro. One cannot say that this will be an essential contribution to fiscal federalism in Austria. Other aspects, such as the gap between responsibility for spending and the responsibility for financing were not touched.

V. Concluding Remarks

Reforms of the federal fiscal system in Austria should strengthen the congruence between spending and revenue responsibilities. One possible alternative would be to give Länder and municipalities the power to generate own tax revenues to a certain extent. The volume of co-funding should be scaled back correspondingly to reduce the adverse incentives generated by the present system.

In preparation of the introduction of such elements of fiscal federalism in the Austrian financial constitution the impacts of fiscal competition in Austria's political system should be however analysed carefully.

The new pact of the financial settlement between the three levels of government in Austria (federal level, Länder and municipalities) has brought no change in the principles of the Austrian Financial Constitution. There are now four further years left to decide, if Austria stays on its traditional path or will go a new way.

ARTHUR GUNLICKS

STATE AND LOCAL GOVERNMENT FINANCE IN THE UNITED STATES

I. Introduction

According to the U.S. Census Bureau, there were 281,422,000 people living in the United States in 2000. As a federation, the country has one federal government, fifty state governments, and, according to the source above, 87,453 local governments categorized as follows:

County	3,043
Municipal (City)	19,372
Township and town	16,629
School district	13,726
Special district	34,683
Total local governments	87,453

Counties, municipalities (cities), and towns are the organizational units in which Americans live. American counties are similar to German *Landkreise* in many ways; however, American counties are not associations of cities and towns (*Gemeindeverbände*), they usually have a large percentage of unincorporated territory, and German-style city-county separation exists as a rule only in Virginia. As a result the proportion of unincorporated land varies widely depending on the density of population in the county, and in some rural counties very little land is incorporated. The municipal governments are generally comparable to *Städte und Gemeinden* in Germany, i.e., they are general purpose *Kommunen*. Townships are primarily rural units of government that are similar to counties in the services they provide and in a few states actually replace the counties. They are found in only 20 states, mostly in the Midwest.

School districts and special districts (*Zweckverbände*) are generally overlapping units of government that provide a distinct service (airports, public housing, parks or sewers, for example) but are not general purpose units of government. School districts are led by separately elected boards; however, municipal and county councils control their financing, together with state authorities.

In any federal system, each level of government has certain sources of revenues, whether basically shared as in Germany or largely own source as in the United States (*Trennsystem*). Federal revenues increased every year from 1969 to 2000, when they reached more than two trillion dollars; however, between 2000 and 2003 they declined steadily to 1.782 trillion. In 2001-2002 about 46 percent of federal revenues were derived from the individual income tax and about 38 percent from social security payments.[1]

II. State Revenues

The fifty American states, unlike the sixteen German *Länder*, have the right to raise their own taxes and, as a result, enjoy considerable tax autonomy. Table 1 lists a variety of revenue sources for the states and local governments. The table also shows that a significant proportion of revenue for state and local governments is derived from intergovernmental transfers, i.e., federal grants-in-aid to the states and local governments and state aid to local governments. According to Table 1, the total amount of federal grants to state and local governments in 2001-2002 was $360,534,000,000 (although the *Book of States*[2] lists the amount of total federal aid for 2002 as a little more than $412 billion).[3] According to the data in Table 1, federal grants amounted to 29.9 percent of total state revenues. This was a higher proportion than usual in recent decades, when federal grants to the states hovered around 26 percent of state general revenue. Thus in 1977 the proportion of federal grants to the states was 27.1 percent, and in 2001 it was 27.5.[4] This stability, especially since 1992, stands in sharp contrast to the dramatic growth of federal grant aid from 1960 to 1973, when inflation-adjusted aid increased 293 percent.[5] The

1 Data from the Congressional Budget Office, Table 1, http://www.cbo.gov/showdoc.cfm?index=1821&sequence=0, accessed 22 November 2004.

2 Book of States 2004, Lexington, Va: Council of State Governments, 2004, p. 41.

3 Data sources on government revenues and expenditures in the United States are sometimes neither consistent nor very current. Different statistical-gathering agencies, e.g., the Census Bureau, the National Association of State Budget Officers, the Council of State Governments, etc., as well as the various states, may use different definitions and accounting methods, so that the consumer of these data must be aware of differences.

4 *Tannenwald, R.*, "Are State and Local Revenue Systems Becoming Obsolete?," Washington, D. C.: National League of Cities, 2004, p. 1.

5 Ibid., pp. 1-2.

per capita grants in 2001-2002 ranged from $4,857 in Alaska to $848 in Nevada.[6]

While Table 1 shows total revenues of the states, it does not, of course, indicate the wide variation in revenues for the individual states. In 2002 the amount of sales tax revenue, for example, ranged from 14 percent (Vermont) to 62.6 percent (Washington) of total general revenues, while the average in the 45 states that have a sales tax[7] was 33.5 percent. The amount received from the state income tax ranged from 17.9 (North Dakota) to 71.5 percent (Oregon) of total general revenues, with an average of 34.7 percent in the 41 states[8] that have a broad-based income tax.[9]

Table 1

STATE AND LOCAL GOVERNMENT REVENUES BY LEVEL OF GOVERNMENT 2001-2002

	State government amount	Local government amount
Revenue*	$1,097,829,366,000	$1,083,129,289,000
General revenue*	$1,062,305,175,000	$995,855,965,000

6 "Virginia Compared to the Other States: National Rankings on Taxes, Budgetary Components, and Other Indicators," Richmond: Joint Legislative Audit and Review Commission, 2004, Item 12.

7 Five states do not have a sales tax: Alaska, Delaware, Montana, New Hampshire, and Oregon.

8 Nine states do not have a broad-based income tax: Alaska, Florida, Nevada, New Hampshire, South Dakota, Tennessee, Texas, Washington, and Wyoming. New Hampshire and Tennessee have very minor, rather than broad-based, income taxes.

9 Tax Policy Center, Urban Institute, Brookings Institution, 2003: http://www.taxpolicycenter.org/TaxFacts/TFDB/TFTemplate.cfm?Docid=310&Topic2id, accessed 19 November 2004.

	State government amount	Local government amount
Intergovernmental revenue*	$335,422,978,000	$398,496,939,000
From federal government	$317,581,354,000	$42,952,953,000
From state government		$355,543,986,000
From local governments*		$17,841,624,000
General revenue from own sources	$726,882,197,000	$597,359,026,000
Taxes	$535,241,161,000	$369,730,209,000
Property	$9,702,385,000	$269,419,295,000
Sales and gross receipts	$262,360,613,000	$61,679,232,000
General sales	$179,665,257,000	$43,321,430,000
Selective sales	$82,695,356,000	$18,357,802,000
Motor fuel	$31,968,036,000	$1,076,213,000
Alcoholic beverage	$4,249,208,000	$350,948,000
Tobacco products	$8,902,018,000	$190,847,000
Public utilities	$10,287,949,000	$10,005,774,000
Other selective sales	$27,288,145,000	$6,734,020,000
Individual income	$185,696,573,000	$17,161,561,000
Corporate income	$25,123,137,000	$3,028,725,000
License taxes	$35,391,102,000	$1,333,522,000
Motor vehicle license	$15,641,246,000	$1,302,673,000
Other taxes	$16,967,351,000	$17,107,874,000

	State government amount	Local government amount
Charges and miscellaneous general revenue	$191,641,036,000	$227,628,817,000
Current charges	$99,810,768,000	$153,381,745,000
Education	$55,166,186,000	$17,234,505,000
Institutions of Higher education	$54,551,798,000	$6,876,731,000
School lunch sales (gross)	$19,342,000	$5,936,660,000
Hospitals	$24,143,857,000	$41,501,554,000
Highways	$5,262,431,000	$3,106,144,000
Air transportation (airports)	$791,614,000	$11,539,001,000
Parking facilities		$1,402,151,000
Sea and inland port facilities	$735,873,000	$1,949,262,000
Natural resources	$2,115,202,000	$850,365,000
Parks and recreation	$1,199,448,000	$5,820,048,000
Housing and Community development	$529,252,000	$3,766,485,000
Sewerage	$33,643,000	$27,055,622,000
Solid waste management	$369,854,000	$10,820,368,000
Other charges	$9,463,408,000	$28,336,240,000
Miscellaneous general revenue	$91,830,268,000	$74,247,072,000
Interest earnings	$31,867,226,000	$35,210,758,000
Special assessments	$118,776,000	$4,660,663,000
Sale of property	$1,001,554,000	$1,348,505,000
Other general revenue	$58,842,712,000	$33,027,246,000

	State government amount	Local government amount
Other than general revenue	$35,524,191,000	$87,273,324,000
Utility revenue	$11,935,400,000	$90,386,981,000
Water supply	$159,309,000	$33,047,385,000
Electric power	$10,102,135,000	$44,301,674,000
Gas supply	$11,743,000	$5,750,002,000
Transit	$1,662,213,000	$7,287,920,000
Liquor store revenue	$4,287,846,000	$777,261,000
Insurance trust revenue	$19,300,945,000	$-3,890,918,000
Unemployment compensation	$26,959,552,000	$125,973,000
Employee retirement	$-25,244,197,000	$-4,016,891,000
Workers' compensation	$13,624,173,000	
Other insurance trust revenue	$3,961,417,000	

*Duplicative intergovernmental transactions are excluded.

Source: U.S. Census Bureau (www.census.gov/govs/estimate/0200ussl_1.html, accessed 21 November 2004).

These differences, of course, are largely the results of different tax rates applied by the states. Thus the state sales tax rate varies from 2.9 percent in Colorado to 7 percent in Mississippi. These state tax rates can be somewhat misleading, however, as they are often combined with local option rates that yield a higher overall rate at the point of sale. For example, when Alabama's 4 percent tax rate is added to the 7 percent local rate, it yields an effective rate of 11 percent in many localities. Virginia's 3.5 percent state sales tax (increased to 4 percent in August 2004) becomes an effective 4.5 percent (now 5 percent) because *all* localities have put in place the local option sales tax.

Another difference is that about 40 percent of the states with sales taxes exempt food items.[10] An especially clear example for many consumers is the tax on tobacco products, with the tax rate per pack of cigarettes ranging from 2.5 cents in Virginia[11] until August 2004 and 3 cents in Kentucky (both important tobacco producing states) to $2.05 in New Jersey. State income tax rates vary from 10 percent in Rhode Island to 3 percent in Illinois; if combined with the *local* income tax raised in eleven states, the highest overall rate of 10.5 percent is found in New York.

State income taxes and the general sales taxes each account for about a quarter of total state own-source revenues. Selective sales taxes, e.g., taxes on tobacco products, alcoholic beverages, and motor fuels, accounted for about 17 percent of the states' own-source revenues in 1977; however, they have declined in importance since then. The heavy reliance on income taxes and general sales taxes has raised concerns about the ability of the states to meet their growing responsibilities. This is especially true of those states that have either no sales tax or no income tax.[12]

Some observers argue that the increasing importance of a service-based economy is having a negative impact on state revenues. The proportion of wages and salaries earned in the goods-producing sector decreased from 1960 to 2002 from 42 to 22 percent, while the proportion earned in private services increased from 16 to 38 percent. During the same period, Americans increased their consumption dollars of services from 41 to 59 percent. These trends have been cited as reasons for concern about the future of the general sales tax as a major source of state revenues.

Others, however, contend that the plausibility of this argument is undermined by the fact that producers of services purchase goods of various kinds that are taxed, that some of these goods were sheltered from sales taxes in the past, and that "the shift in production from tax-sheltered to broadly taxable sectors has actually bolstered state and local sales tax bases."[13] It should also be noted that efforts to tax services have not been successful in the recent past and remain difficult to achieve because of the political influence of the professional

---

10 Ibid., http://www.taxpolicycenter.org/TaxFacts/TFDB/TFTemplate.cfm?Docid=245&Topic2id, accessed 19 November 2004.

11 The rate in Virginia was increased to 20 cents a pack in August 2004 and will be increased to 30 cents in July 2005.

12 *Tannenwald*, pp. 3-5.

13 Ibid., p. 7.

service groups that would be subject to the tax. Only three states do tax a wide array of services.[14]

Nevertheless, the ratio of taxable sales to gross state product has declined from 39.5 percent in 1977 to 34.9 percent in 2001. However, this decline is the result not only of the growing share of consumption of services but is also a consequence of a gradual expansion of sales tax exemptions. In addition it can be argued that cyclical factors in the economy have influenced the role of sales taxes. Thus taxed consumption has increased more than tax exempt consumption over the past 35 years.[15]

What is a greater challenge for states and their sales tax revenues is electronic commerce. Enforcement of state laws assessing taxes on e-commerce has been found to be difficult, and court decisions regarding state and local taxation of mail-order sales have ruled that making the sellers responsible for collecting the tax impedes the flow of interstate commerce and is therefore unconstitutional. While there are some observers who suggest that new tax software and certain reforms of the state and local tax systems might contain the potential loss of revenues due to e-commerce, others have predicted that from 2001 to 2006 states will lose from 1 to 3 percent of total state revenues to the growth of e-commerce. There are also questions regarding the impact of e-commerce on the state corporate income taxes.[16] John Kincaid has noted that the inability of states to tax out-of-state Internet and catalog sales may have cost them $20 billion in 2001-2002. But he notes that representatives of 34 states negotiated a Streamlined Sales Tax agreement that holds some promise of relief. Pressure is now on state legislatures to enact the agreement.[17]

Finally, there are increasing concerns about competition among the states and their local governments and from abroad. There are some arguments that a certain level of competition is beneficial, but others note that it "'has escalated into a bidding crescendo that is injuring the winners as well as the losers.'"[18] States and local governments are, of course, under great pressure to attract and maintain jobs for their citizens, and it is clear that subnational fiscal competition has intensified. All states have increased incentives over the years, and employers report that they have been offered increased incentives in comparison to five years ago. Tennessee offered Nissan a package of incentives worth

14 Ibid., p. 9.

15 Ibid., pp. 10-15.

16 Ibid., pp. 23-26.

17 *Kincaid, J.*, "Trends in Federalism: Continuity, Change and Polarization," Book of the States, Lexingtron: Council of State Governments, 2004, p. 23.

18 Cited in *Tannenwald*, p. 27.

about $11,000 per job in 1980, Alabama offered Daimler Benz $168,000 per job in 1993, and other states have offered far more per job in more recent years. One result has apparently been a decline in the percentage of corporate profits subject to the corporate income tax. New York City reported in 2002 that it had lost more than $550 million in property tax revenues and in 1999 that it lost about 12 percent of business profit revenues. In the meantime, the ratio of state and local personal taxes and charges to personal income has risen over the years.[19]

III. Local Government Revenues

As we saw in Table 1 above, the general sales tax and personal income tax are the most important revenue sources for the states; for the local governments, the property tax is the most important own source of revenue. It represented 73 percent of all local tax revenue in 2002 and 45 percent of all own source revenue. The second most important own source of revenue, user charges, is about 38 percent of all own source revenue. In 2001-2002 the property tax was 25 percent of the total of all revenues, including state and federal grants. That same year state grants accounted for 35.6 percent of the local general revenue total, and federal grants added another 4.3 percent. State aid to school districts has been especially important, reaching 54 percent of total school district revenue in 1997. This exceeds the property tax revenues (36 percent in 1977), which are the most important own source for school districts.[20]

Table 2 shows the total revenues, including state and federal aid, of the different kinds of local governments in 1997. The great importance of state aid and of the property tax for own source revenues is clear. The reliance of local governments on the property tax (real estate tax or *Realsteuer*) was a factor in the "property tax revolt" represented in 1978 by "Proposition 13" in California and later by the less radical "Proposition 2 ½" in Massachusetts. These revolts have placed major constraints on the states and encouraged them to turn more to local sales taxes and even to income taxes in larger cities.[21]

State aid is a very important part of local revenue, and it varies widely among the states. It has been fairly constant nationwide since 1977, but there has been a slight rising trend from 1987 to 2000. It has declined in some states in the past three decades, and since 1982 state aid to local governments has grown

19 Ibid., pp. 27-30.
20 Ibid., pp. 3-4.
21 Ibid., p. 5.

more slowly than state spending as a whole. As a result, there is considerable uncertainty about the level of state aid in the future.[22]

Table 2

LOCAL GENERAL REVENUES BY SOURCE AND TYPE OF GOVERNMENT 1997

	Counties	Municipalities	Townships*	School Districts	Special Districts
Federal grants	3.0%	5.0%	1.0%	1.0%	15.0%
State grants	33.0%	21.0%	20.0%	54.0%	9.0%
Other	13.0%	22.0%	12.0%	5.0%	21.0%
Property taxes	25.0%	21.0%	56.0%	36.0%	12.0%
Sales taxes	6.0%	7.0%	0.0%	0.0%	3.0%
User fees/ charges	19.0%	19.0%	9.0%	4.0%	40.0%
Income taxes	1.0%	5.0%	2.0%	0.0%	0.0%

*Primarily rural units of government that are similar to counties in the services they provide. They are found in only 20 states, mostly in the Midwest.

Source: Robert Tannenwald, "Are State Revenue Systems Becoming Obsolete?" Washington, D. C.: National League of Cities, 2004, p. 3.

22 Ibid.

IV. State Expenditures

Table 3 provides a detailed listing of expenditures of state and local governments in 2001-2002. The economic downturn that began even before the 9/11 terrorist attack (which exacerbated the problem), declining federal funds, antiquated tax structures, rising health care costs and other factors forced the states to make many painful choices "in a time characterized by many as the worst fiscal crisis since WWII."[23] In 2002 states cut almost $14 billion from their planned expenditures. Forty states made cuts of $12 billion in 2003, with 21 states ending the year with negative spending growth. Thirty-two states made across-the-board budget cuts, 25 took money from their reserve funds, 16 laid off employees, 13 offered early retirement, and 13 reorganized programs.[24] For 2004 three-fourths of the states imposed new taxes and fee increases, cut spending, and further reduced their reserve funds.[25] The National Conference of State Legislatures has warned that states can expect a budget gap in 2005 of about $35 billion. This is somewhat less than in 2004, but the problem is exacerbated by the fact that the states have exhausted many of the funds or strategies used to keep state programs operating.[26]

Table 3

STATE AND LOCAL GOVERNMENT EXPENDITURES
2001-2002

	State government amount	Local government amount
Expenditures*	$1,280,290,224,000	$1,140,082,069,000
Intergovernmental expenditure*	$364,789,480,000	$11,251,601,000

23 *Willoughby*, K. G., "Tax Revenues in 2004: Governors Look Inward?" Book of the States, Lexington: Council of State Governments, 2004, p. 325.

24 *Nick Samuels*, "Long-Term Budget Stability Amidst Fiscal Crisis: What Can States Do to Better Navigate the Next One?" in Ibid., p. 330.

25 *Willoughby*, p. 325.

26 Ibid., pp. 327-328.

	State government amount	Local government amount
Direct expenditure	$915,500,744,000	$1,128,830,468,000
Current operations	$620,762,606,000	$876,453,756,000
Capital outlay	$89,919,022,000	$167,294,636,000
Construction	$71,034,814,000	$126,594,303,000
Other capital outlay	$18,884,208,000	$40,700,333,000
Assistance and subsidies	$24,313,447,000	$8,968,367,000
Interest on debt	$33,219,770,000	$53,727,795,000
Insurance benefits and repayments	$147,285,899,000	$22.385,914,000
Exhibit: Salaries and wages	$169,045,937,000	$441,832,842,000
Direct expenditure by function	$915,500,744,000	$1,128,830,468,000
Direct general expenditure	$744,437,968,000	$968,370,919,000
Capital outlay	$84,765,874,000	$142,209,210,000
Other direct general expenditure	$659,672,094,000	$844,161,709,000
Education services		
Education	$162,054,012,000	$432,536,659,000
Higher education	$131,281,585,000	$25,528,667,000
Elementary and secondary	$4,064,934,000	$407,007,992,000
Other education	$26,707,493,000	
Libraries	$419,049,000	$7,838,059,000

	State government amount	Local government amount
Social services and income maintenance		
Public welfare	$239,903,027,000	$39,694,663,000
Cash assistance payments	$10,650,907,000	$8,968,367,000
Vendor payments	$190,809,064,000	$3,105,295,000
Other public welfare	$38,443,056,000	$27,621,001.000
Hospitals	$36,965,012,000	$50,282,325,000
Health	$29,837,067,000	$29,295,174,000
Social insurance administration	$5,072,948,000	$9,182,000
Veterans' services	$361,190,000	
Transportation		
Highways	$71,248,101,000	$44,219,354,000
Air transportation (airports)	$1,170,391,000	$15,038,851,000
Parking facilities		$1,122,848,000
Sea and inland port facilities	$1,014,880,000	$2,556,172,000
Transit subsidies	$304,225,000	$321,344,000
Public safety		
Police protection	$9,407,598,000	$55,084,296,000
Fire protection		$25,977,992,000
Correction	$36,471,670,000	$18,215,499,000
Protective inspection and regulation	$7,873,548,000	$3,755,502,000

	State government amount	Local government amount
Environment and housing		
Natural resources	$16,588,299,000	$5,411,890,000
Parks and recreation	$4,952,534,000	$25,143,156,000
Housing and community development	$3,783,028,000	$27,827,442,000
Sewerage	$1,049,804,000	$30,188,682,000
Solid waste management	$2,736,496,000	$16,310,997,000
Governmental administration		
Financial administration	$18,941,877,000	$13,711,331,000
Judicial and legal	$14,415,793,000	$16,820,018,000
General public buildings	$2,632,930,000	$8,264,415,000
Other governmental administration	$3,921,391,000	$14,081,742,000
Interest on general debt	$31,426,313,000	$43,876,356,000
General expenditure, n.e.c.		
Miscellaneous commercial activities	$360,176,000	$59,245,000
Other and unallocable	$41,526,609,000	$58,727,725,000
Utility expenditure	$20,278,852,000	$119,388,838,000
Water supply	$386,106,000	$40,140,839,000
Electric power	$11,688,979,000	$44,263,358,000
Gas supply	$8,929,000	$5,711,206,000
Transit	$8,194,838,000	$29,273,435,000

	State government amount	Local government amount
Liquor store expenditure	$3,498,025,000	$684,797,000
Insurance trust expenditure	$147,285,899,000	$22,385,914.000
Unemployment compensation	$42,016,889,000	$149,476,000
Employee retirement	$91,971,465,000	$22,236,438,000
Workers' compensation	$9,784,639,000	
Other insurance trust	$3,512,906,000	
Debt outstanding	$642,202,068,000	$1,043,904,090,000
Cash and security holdings	$2,534,038,898,000	$1,095,364,284,000

Source: U.S. Census Bureau (www.census.gov/govs/estimate/0200ussl_1.html, accessed 21 November 2004).

In spite of bad news on the fiscal front after 2001, the situation appeared to be improving by the end of 2004. Only eight states had to increase taxes in 2004 to balance their budgets, which is probably a sign that the states' fiscal squeeze may finally be over. The states that did raise taxes increased their taxes by a total of $2.6 billion in 2004, considerably less than the $7 billion states raised from higher taxes in 2003. In five states the legislatures raised taxes, while in the other three referenda were passed. In most cases the taxes raised were on tobacco products.[27]

As indicated in Table 4 below, state spending in the past three years has been over one trillion dollars, including both operating and capital expenditures. This represents an increase of 1.4 percent in state funds and an increase of 10.3 percent in federal funds for a total of 4.5 percent from 2002 to 2003; for 2003 to 2004, estimates are for an increase of 2.4 and 9.9 percent increases in

27 *Prah, P. M.*, "Eight states raised taxes in 2004," Stateline.org, accessed 23 November 2004.

state and federal funds, respectively, also for a total of 4.5 percent (see Table 5).

Table 4

STATE EXPENDITURES
2002-2004

	2002	2003	2004 (estimated)
General Fund	$499,051,000	$499,425,000,000	$516,095,000,000
Federal Funds	$295,752,000	$326,239,000,000	$358,417,000,000
Other State Funds	$265,918,000	$276,054,000,000	$277,621,000,000
Bonds	$27,486,000	$34,976,000,000	$35,311,000,000
Total	$1,088,207,000	$1,136,694,000,000	$1,187,444,000,000

Source: "2003 State Expenditure Report," National Association of State Budget Officers, p. 6.

The role of federal grant money can be seen in Table 5 below. These funds were contained in 608 categorical grants and 17 block grants for state and local governments. Federal funds were 11.2 percent of elementary and secondary education funds and 4.8 percent of higher education funds in 2004; however, their importance stands out in the aid they provide for Medicaid, the federal-state program that covers health care costs of those who fall below a minimum income set by the states.

Table 5

ANNUAL PERCENTAGE CHANGE IN TOTAL STATE EXPENDITURES
2002-2004

	From 2002 to 2003	From 2003 to 2004
State Funds	1.4%	2.4%
Federal Funds	10.3%	9.9%
All Funds	4.5%	4.5%

Source: "2003 State Expenditure Report," National Association of State Budget Officers, p. 7.

Table 6

COMPARISON OF SHARES OF STATE SPENDING WITH FUND SOURCE 1994-2004 (2004 IN PARENTHESES)

	General Funds	Other State Funds	Federal Funds	Bond Funds	Total Funds
Elementary and Secondary Education	34.9% (35.2%)	9.0% (9.2%)	10.2% (11.2%)	15.6% (20.7%)	21.6 (21.5%)
Higher Education	12.6% (11.5%)	13.8% (15.0%)	4.1% (4.8%)	19.6% (18.4%)	10.8% (10.5%)
Public Assistance	3.1% (2.3%)	0.5% (0.3%)	4.9% (3.4%)	0.0% (0.0%)	2.9% (2.1%)
Medicaid	15.0% (16.5%)	6.4% (7.3%)	43.2% (43.1%)	0.0% (0.0%)	20.2% (21.9%)
Corrections	6.8% (7.0%)	0.9% (0.8%)	0.3% (0.4%)	6.0% (2.7%)	3.6% (3.4%)
Transportations and Highways	0.8% (0.7%)	22.0% (19.4%)	9.1% (8.2%)	25.7% (21.1%)	8.7% (7.9%)
All Other	26.7% (26.8%)	47.3% (48.0%)	28.2% (28.8%)	33.2% (37.0%)	32.2% (32.6%)
Total (100.0%)	100.0% (100.0%)	100.0% (100.0%)	100.0% (100.0%)	100.0% (100.0%)	100.0% (100.0%)

Source: "2003 State Expenditure Report," National Association of State Budget Officers, p. 8.

In Table 4 and Table 6 above, "Bonds" and "Bond Funds" are included. States and local governments generally are required to meet operating expenses from general revenues, but they may issue short term "tax-anticipation notes" when revenues have not yet been collected. States and local governments may borrow funds (*Kredite*) for capital improvements, such as roads, highways, school and university buildings, or civic centers, usually as a result of a referendum passed by the voters. Other bonds may be sold to build facilities such as toll bridges, toll roads, university dormitories, or football stadiums that can be expected to generate revenues that, in turn, can be used to repay the bondholders.[28] States have gained different reputations over the years for their repayment discipline. They are rated by a bonding agency for the quality of their bonds, and the rating affects the interest the states must pay their bondholders. Otherwise states – except Vermont – are required by law to balance their operating budgets. In the case of California, budgets are to be balanced in the coming years with the help of a $15 billion bond issue approved by the voters in 2004. Thus rather than raising taxes, Governor Schwarzenegger appears to be counting on the principle of hope and a growing economy to help him with his deficits.

State governments are under great financial pressure in general, but a – if not the – primary reason is the growing cost Medicaid, the free federal-state health insurance program for persons of low income mentioned above. This program now consumes 45 percent of all federal grant money and represents the best example of what John Kincaid calls a shift in federal aid during the past few decades from place-based functions, such as economic development, transportation, crime and justice, and government operations, to persons. On the other hand, Homeland Security costs following 9/11 are now also causing fiscal problems. In response Congress passed a $20 billion package of aid in 2003 for the next fiscal year, with $10 billion for Medicaid and $10 billion as a "flexible grant."[29] Other than Homeland Security, changes that have occurred in the provision of aid to places have largely been the result of pork-barrel politics. Thus projects earmarked for aid increased from 2000 in 1998 to 9362 in 2003.[30]

An old problem in the relations between the federal and state governments, as in Germany, is unfunded mandates. This was supposedly fixed by the Unfunded Mandate Reform Act of 1995, but critics argue that Homeland Security, Medicaid, the No Child Left Behind Act, and special education programs are *underfunded* de facto mandates.[31] States are complaining about the costs of these programs, but there is little hope for additional federal aid at this time.

---

28 *Harrigan, J. J./Nice, D. C.*, Politics and Policy in States and Communities, 8th ed., New York: Pearson Longman, 2004, pp. 316-317.

29 *Kincaid*, p. 22.

30 Ibid., pp. 22-23.

31 Ibid., p. 23.

V. Reform Proposals

There has been no significant change in the proportions the major revenue sources have provided the states during the past ten years. Table 7 below shows the continuing dominance of the general sales tax and individual income tax as the major sources for the states from 1994 to 2004. The proportion of total revenues provided by general sales taxes has decreased somewhat and the proportion provided by the individual income tax has increased slightly, but other changes, except for "other taxes," have been modest.

Table 7

STATE TAX COLLECTIONS BY TYPE OF TAX
1994 AND 2003, 3rd QUARTER

	1994	2003
General Sales and Gross receipts	34.6%	31.4%
Individual income tax	31.5%	33.1%
Motor fuel sales	7.1%	6.3%
Corporate net income	6.6%	5.0%
Motor vehicles	3.3%	3.0%
Other sales and gross receipts	2.3%	2.5%
Tobacco products	2.0%	2.1%
Insurance	2.0%	1.9%
All other taxes (property tax, public utilities, Pari-mutuels, amusements, beverage and other licenses, death, gift and severance tax, and taxes on documents and stock transactions)	10.4%	14.7%

Source: Katherine G. Wollougby, "Tax Revenues in 2004: Governors Look Inward?" Book of the States, Lexington: Council of State Governments, 2004, p. 328.

Table 7 does show, however, that revenues from general sales taxes are declining, and we have seen that there is growing concern about the future yield from this important source. As noted above, some observers point to the growing service sector and declining good-producing sector as reasons to apply the sales tax to services. Others object that this would discriminate against businesses that rely heavily on services, or they note that efforts to tax professional services are severely handicapped by the political influence of professional groups. Sales tax exemptions for certain goods could be reduced, but this would create new distortions in favor of vertically integrated businesses that are not affected by the pyramiding of the tax as it is applied to successive stages of production. Tax simplification that would create uniform taxes among local governments might be a strategy with some promise, but it would be difficult to achieve and would undermine the autonomy of local governments.

Controls on the competition for investments and jobs could help lessen the self-destructive business incentives that are being offered by the states and local governments, but these would probably have to come from the courts and/or federal government. This would in any case be highly controversial and would do nothing to protect subnational governments from foreign competition. One study recommends that at least state "right-to-know" laws requiring more information for the public about the incentives being offered and the costs entailed and "clawback" provisions which require businesses that receive incentives to meet certain conditions or repay the subsidies should become standard parts of any offer.[32]

One could argue that taxes in the American states would be fairer if there were more reliance on the individual income tax rather than the more regressive sales taxes. But the general anti-tax pressures that persist in the American political culture have made state legislators very wary of imposing new taxes of any kind. This is especially the case since the tax revolts against property taxes in California in 1978 and Massachusetts in 1980. On the other hand, states have found it easier politically to sell various sales taxes, e.g., cigarette taxes, in order to secure badly needed revenues. The continuing failure of referenda to reform state tax systems, e.g., in Alabama and Oregon in 2003 and 2004, and the recall of Governor Gray Davis in California and his replacement by Arnold Schwarzenegger in the fall of 2003 are also serious warning signs for state politicians. On the other hand, Virginia was able in 2004 to increase its general sales tax, cigarette tax, and state income tax for higher brackets,

---

32 *Tannenwald*, pp. 31-34.

while making some tax reductions in other areas; however, this was achieved only with the cooperation of the Democratic governor and a number of Republican legislators in the Republican-dominated state legislature, a model that would be difficult to reproduce in most states. Overall, it seems safe to predict that states will continue to hope for improvements in the economy as the major source of improvement in their tax revenues, while making minor changes in taxes in order to meet more immediate needs.

III. COMPETENCIES AND POWERS

JEAN LECLAIR

REFORMING THE DIVISION OF POWERS IN CANADA: AN (UN)ACHIEVABLE ENDEAVOUR ?[1]

Formal amendments to the division of powers provisions of Canada's 1867 federal constitution[2] have always proved difficult to achieve. However, since 1982, this task has become hopelessly unachievable. Modifications to, and adaptation of, the division of powers has consequently been left to judges called upon to interpret sections 91 to 95 of the *Constitution Act, 1867* and to executives officers of the central and regional governments as they negotiate intergovernmental agreements. The end result of these two processes has been highly favourable to the central government. Courts have given a liberal interpretation to the central government's exclusive fields of jurisdiction. Moreover, the latter's spending power, unobstructed by the fragile legal framework imposed under interprovincial agreements, has enabled it to encroach upon the exclusive heads of power of the provinces.

As we will see, one of the main reasons behind the Canadian constitutional stalemate, and for the recurrent isolation of Québec – even where informal modifications are concerned – is the different conceptions of Canadian federalism respectively held by Quebecers and by English Canadians.

I. Formal Amendments to the Division of Powers

Canada's 1867 federal constitution is the fourth written constitution enacted by the British Parliament for the better administration of its North American colonies. Adopted at the request of three of the six British North American colonies then in existence, the Act had as its purpose the unification of those colonies in one federal country.[3] The wish to find a way out of the economic crisis of the 1850s by creating a common market and the desire to put an end to the political and constitutional difficulties of the United Province of Canada (comprised of what would become in 1867 the provinces of Ontario and Qué-

1 Paper delivered at the workshop "Reforming Federalism – Foreign Experiences for a Reform in Germany" hosted by the Institute for Legal Policy (University of Trier, Germany) and the German Bundesrat, December 2nd-4th, 2004.

2 Sections 91 to 95, reproduced in Annex A of this paper.

3 Between 1867 and 1949, other colonies joined the federation, and provinces were also created out of federal territories (*Morin & Woehrling* 1994: 401-408). Canada now comprises 10 provinces and 3 territories.

bec) were the main impetus for the adoption of the *British North America Act, 1867*, now known as the *Constitution Act 1867*.

Although a legislative union would have been the preferred choice of many English Canadians, the staunch opposition of the French Canadians made federalism the only politically realistic choice. Indeed, federalism enabled them to form a majority in Québec and thus control the legislature and, more importantly, their collective destiny. In the words of *Thomas Courchene*, "Quebec's gift to Canada was federalism" (*2004: 21*). The Supreme Court of Canada has recently emphasized that fact (*Re Secession of Quebec 1998: ¶59*):

> The principle of federalism facilitates the pursuit of collective goals by cultural and linguistic minorities which form the majority within a particular province. This is the case in Quebec, where the majority of the population is French-speaking, and which possesses a distinct culture. This is not merely the result of chance. The social and demographic reality of Quebec explains the existence of the province of Quebec as a political unit and indeed, was one of the essential reasons for establishing a federal structure for the Canadian union in 1867. The experience of both Canada East and Canada West under the *Union Act, 1840* (U.K.), 3-4 Vict., c. 35, had not been satisfactory. The federal structure adopted at Confederation enabled French-speaking Canadians to form a numerical majority in the province of Quebec, and so exercise the considerable provincial powers conferred by the *Constitution Act, 1867* in such a way as to promote their language and culture. It also made provision for certain guaranteed representation within the federal Parliament itself.

Today this principle continues to be of particular significance to Québec. One of Canada's ten provinces, Québec is the place of residence of 23.6% of the Canadian population[4] and, more importantly, the home land of 85% of Canada's francophone community.[5] It is also the only territory in Canada where private law is administered under a civil law system.

---

4 According to the 2004 Census of population – Statistics Canada, the percentage of population of the provinces and territories is as follows:
- Atlantic Canada: Newfoundland and Labrador: 1.6%; Prince Edward Island: 0.4%; Nova Scotia: 2.9% and New Brunswick: 2.4%.
- Central Canada: Quebec: 23.6% and Ontario: 38.8%.
- Western Canada: Manitoba: 3.7%; Saskatchewan: 3.1%; Alberta: 10% and British Columbia: 13.1%.
- Federal Territories: Yukon: 0.1%; Northwest Territories: 0.1% and Nunavut: 0.1%.

5 2001 Census of population – Statistics Canada – Mother Tongue, 2001 Counts for Both Sexes, for Canada, Provinces and Territories. Within Quebec, the mother tongue of the population is as follows: 81.2% French; 8% English; 0.8% French and English and 10% another language than French or English.

Coming back to 1867, notwithstanding the importance of the "francophone factor", for many English Canadians at the time, "federalism was at best a regrettable concession imposed by Québec and, to a lesser degree, the Maritimes" (*McRoberts 1997: 10*). Therefore, since "more than one spirit presided at the deliberations that led to Confederation" (*id.: 11*), it is no wonder that the Constitution of 1867 was an ambiguous text with a mixture of centralist and decentralist features, where the former nevertheless predominated (*Hogg & Wright 2004*).

In dividing powers between the central and provincial levels of government, the Fathers of Confederation intended the central government to be endowed with the power to regulate matters of general concern (section 91). In particular, these included all matters that affected Canada's economic life. In addition, the constitution of 1867 granted the central government exclusive access to the most important source of revenue at the time, indirect taxes.

As for the provinces, they were awarded the power to regulate matters generally seen as local in scope (section 92). Incidentally, these matters directly concerned Québec's distinctive cultural institutions: education, civil law, solemnization of marriage, and so on. Provincial sources of revenue were limited to direct taxes and the profit reaped from the exploitation of the public domain's natural resources.

Finally, some sections of the 1867 constitution specifically recognised Québec's special status in the federation. Section 94 for instance bestowed on Parliament, under certain conditions, the ability to legislate over property and civil rights – a provincial head of power – in all provinces, except Québec:

> [The] Parliament of Canada may make Provision for the Uniformity of all or any of the Laws relative to Property and Civil Rights in Ontario, Nova Scotia, and New Brunswick, and of the Procedure of all or any of the Courts in those Three provinces [...]; but any Act of the Parliament of Canada making Provision for such Uniformity shall not have effect in any Province unless and until it is adopted and enacted as Law by the Legislature thereof.

This section – to which Parliament has never resorted – was meant to protect Québec's civil law heritage, that province being the only one with such a legal system.

Sections 91 and 92 expressly grant each level of government the exclusive power to legislate in relation to certain specific matters. The courts were quick to recognise that, because of this exclusivity of legislative jurisdiction, the failure by one level of government to exercise one of its powers under the constitution does not authorise the other level to do so in its stead. The legislative powers distributed under sections 91 and 92 of the Act are said to be "mutually exclusive", therefore guaranteeing the autonomy of both levels of government, more particularly that of the provinces.[6] However, it is also agreed that sections 91 and 92 recognise the existence of classes of law, not of facts. Those sections grant exclusive legislative jurisdiction in relation to certain matters within the enumerated classes of subjects, but it is not the matters or subjects themselves that are granted. Instead, this exclusivity refers to the kinds of legislative purposes that can be fulfilled by exercising a given power. Envisaged in such a manner, the exclusivity principle does not prevent the two orders of government from legislating over the same issue.

According to the "aspect" doctrine developed by the courts, "a law which is federal in its true nature will be upheld even if it affects matters which appear to be a proper subject for provincial legislation (and vice versa)" (*General Motors 1989: 670*). This approach encourages the "overlap of legislation" (*id.*: *669*) rather than compartmentalisation. As long as the main object – or dominant characteristic – of a provincial statute is to achieve a legislative purpose that falls within one of the heads of power listed in section 92 of the constitution, the statute will not be found unconstitutional even if it has a slight impact on an area of federal law. The question of whether the statute also has a federal aspect becomes irrelevant. Conversely, a federal statute whose main purpose is within the legislative authority of Parliament under section 91 of the constitution is not unconstitutional simply because it may affect an area of provincial authority.

What happens, though, when a statute relates to a subject that falls under a head of federal jurisdiction when looked at from one angle and a head of provincial jurisdiction when looked at from another angle? In such a case, the courts say that the subject has a "double aspect." Legislation on broad subjects such as pollution, for example, can therefore be passed by either Parliament or a province, in so far as each is pursuing a purpose that lies within its jurisdiction.

The aspect doctrine and its corollary, the double aspect doctrine, are both the expression of a certain form of judicial deference. The courts generally favour an approach that enables statutes to be found constitutional. When the double aspect doctrine is applied, federal and provincial norms relating to the same subject can both subsist. To resolve the conflicts that may result from the si-

---

6 Nevertheless, there are exceptions to the exclusivity principle. Some jurisdictions are expressly said to be concurrent: agriculture and immigration (s. 95), old age pensions (s. 94A) and export from one province to another of the primary production from non-renewable natural resources and forestry resources (s. 92A (2) and (3)).

multaneous application of the statutes in question, the courts apply the rule of federal paramountcy, according to which any provincial statute that conflicts with a federal statute becomes inoperative.

However, the aspect doctrine may not serve to endanger the rule of exclusive jurisdiction explicitly recognised in sections 91 and 92 of the constitution. It must not deny that exclusivity. On the contrary, it "can only be invoked when it gives effect to the rule of exclusive fields of jurisdiction." (*Bell Canada 1988: 766*) Thus, it can be applied only when the multiplicity of aspects is real. (*id.*) In *Bell Canada 1988* (*id.*), *Beetz J.* noted that the double aspect doctrine must be applied with caution:

> The reason for this caution is the extremely broad wording of the exclusive legislative powers listed in ss. 91 and 92 of the Constitution Act, 1867 and the risk that these two fields of exclusive powers will be combined into a single more or less concurrent field of powers governed solely by the rule of paramountcy of federal legislation.

The courts have played a determining role, not only in fashioning interpretative tools such as the "aspect doctrine" just described, but also in defining the scope of the provincial and central government's respective jurisdictions. Although an expansive interpretation was initially given to the provincial heads of power by the Judicial Committee of the Privy Council to which appeals could be made until 1949 (*Cairns 1971*; *Hogg & Wright 2004*; *Hogg 2005*), it now appears that the pendulum is swinging toward the federation. Indeed, over the last thirty years, the Supreme Court of Canada has clearly been in the process of reinforcing Ottawa's power over the economy (*Leclair 2003*).

First, whenever the opportunity has arisen, the Supreme Court has given a generous interpretation to Parliament's *enumerated* powers. It did so by resorting to purely technical or functional tests which have great centripetal potential (*id.*). Nevertheless, none of these powers allowed for broad federal intervention in the field of commerce, especially at the intraprovincial level. Indeed, Parliament's trade and commerce power (ss. 91(2)) had always been interpreted to allow the Central government to regulate interprovincial and international trade, and to regulate intraprovincial transactions only to the extent that it was necessarily incidental to the effective regulation of interprovincial and international trade. And so, the second and most important reform initiated by the Supreme Court was the recognition to Parliament of a power over the regulation of "general trade and commerce affecting Canada as a whole" (*General Motors 1989*). This new power enabled Parliament, under certain conditions, to adopt legislation "concerned with trade as a whole rather than with a particular industry" (*id.*: *661*). What it conferred on the Central government was jurisdiction over both the interprovincial and the intraprovincial aspects of trade (*Leclair 2003*). Finally, the Supreme Court enhanced Parliament's *residual power*, by giving a liberal interpretation to the "national interest" doctrine (*Zellerbach 1988*). According to that doctrine, when a subject matter is judicially found to have a "national dimension", it thereafter falls within Parliament's permanent and exclusive jurisdiction, pursuant to the residual power set out in the opening words of section 91 of the constitution of 1867. The main virtue of the doctrine is that the power it confers extends to both the interprovincial and the intraprovincial aspects of the subject matter (*Leclair 1993*; *Leclair 2004*).[7]

Consequently, the division of powers between the federal and provincial governments has been modified informally through judicial interpretation and, as we will see in part 2 of this paper, through the exercise of Ottawa's spending power.

This is not to say that the division of powers has never been formally modified since 1867. Three such amendments did occur (in 1940, 1951 and 1982) but they were the product of very special circumstances. The first added unemployment insurance to the central government's list of exclusive powers (s. 91(2A)), whereas the second allocated to Parliament a concurrent power to make laws in relation to old age pensions (s. 94A). Most importantly for our present purposes, these two formal amendments were not controversial; they were agreed to by the federal government and all the provinces, including Québec. As for the third amendment concerning provincial regulation and taxation of natural resources (s. 92A), it was part and parcel of a constitutional package adopted in 1982, about which more will be said in the next paragraph. The purpose of this last amendment was rather limited, since its design was to attenuate the impact of two controversial Supreme Court of Canada decisions that had jeopardized the provinces' ability to regulate the natural resources sector (*Tremblay 1995: 4-6*). Up until 1982, Canada was not empowered to modify its own constitution. And so these 1940, 1951 and 1982 amendments were performed by the British Parliament at the request of the Canadian authorities (federal and provincial).

When initially adopted, the Constitution of 1867 did not contain an amending formula. Being a British colony, no one at the time thought it necessary to provide for such a mechanism. In truth, "the Canadian framers of the B.N.A. Act were content for the imperial Parliament to play a part in the proc-

7 In recent years, the Court has distanced itself form this generous and invasive interpretation of Parliament's residual power (*Leclair* 2003 and 2004).

ess of amending the new Constitution" (*Hogg 2003: 3*). In 1931, the *Statute of Westminster* confirmed the sovereign status of the Canadian state by granting the latter the power, which it had lacked prior to that date, to repeal or amend imperial statutes to which it was then subject. Because no agreement could be struck between Ottawa and the provinces over an amending formula, subsection 7(1) of the Statute provided that "[n]othing in this Act shall be deemed to apply to the repeal, amendment or alteration of the British North America Acts, 1867 to 1930, or any order, rule or regulation made thereunder." In the following decades, the provinces and the Federation met several times to try and agree on a particular formula, but all in vain. Consequently, until 1982, the task of formally amending our constitution therefore fell upon the English Parliament. Constitutional conventions – "constitutional rules which are not binding in any strict sense (that is in a legal sense) but which have come to be recognised and accepted in practice as part of the amendment process in Canada" (*Re: Resolution to Amend the Constitution 1981: 900*) – regulated the manner in which the Canadian authorities could seize London with a demand for constitutional reform.

Eventually, in 1982, Ottawa and all the provinces – with the important exception of Québec – agreed on the amending formula now enshrined in Part V of the *Constitution Act, 1982*.[8] The constitution of 1982 was adopted by the British Parliament at the request of the federal government and the nine English Canadian provinces.[9] In 1981, the Supreme Court of Canada had concluded that, according to the conventions of the Constitution, an amendment to the distribution of legislative power did not require the unanimous consent of all the provinces. "[A] substantial measure of provincial consent" was said to be sufficient for an amendment to proceed (*Re: Resolution to Amend the Constitution 1981: 905*). Québec's opposition was therefore no obstacle to the patriation of the constitution (*Quebec Veto Reference 1982)*.

However, as demonstrated by the failure of the 1987 *Meech Lake Accord* and the 1992 *Charlottetown Accord* – both designed in part to reintegrate Québec within the constitutional family by recognising its cultural specificity[10] – the

---

8 Reproduced in Annex B of this paper.

9 It provided for the repeal of ss. 7(1) of the *Statute of Westminster*.

10 For more information about these two agreements, see *Morin & Woehrling* 1994: 543-577.

cumbersome mechanism established by the amending formula of the constitution of 1982 now renders major constitutional reforms impossible.[11]

A demonstration of this assertion requires a short description of the mechanisms put in place under Part V of the Constitution Act, 1982. Subsection 38(1) of the constitution of 1982 first establishes a general mechanism – a default mechanism – that does not require the unanimous consent of all provinces for an amendment to proceed. According to this provision an amendment to the Constitution may be made by proclamation issued by the Governor General under the Great Seal of Canada. This proclamation must first be authorized by resolutions of the Senate and the House of Commons and by resolutions of the legislative assemblies *of at least two-thirds of the provinces that have, according to the then latest general census, at least fifty per cent of the population of all the provinces*. Any amendment to the division of powers is subject to this general provision. Nevertheless, where such an amendment is concerned, ss. 38(2) further provides that a resolution *supported by a majority of the members* – as opposed to a majority of those present and voting – of each of the Senate, the House of Commons and the legislative assemblies required under subsection (1) is mandated.[12] Hence, an amendment to the division of powers does not require the unanimous consent of the provinces. However, s. 41 does require such unanimity for the amendment of five specific features of the Canadian constitutional order.[13]

---

11 Although, pursuant to s. 43 of the Constitution Act, 1982, amendments to the Constitution of Canada in relation to any provision that applies to one or more, but not all, provinces have proven possible: see *Hogg* 2003: 7; footnote 28.

12 Ss. 38(3) and s. 40 also establish an "opting-out with compensation" mechanism:
38(3). An amendment referred to in subsection (2) shall not have effect in a province the legislative assembly of which has expressed its dissent thereto by resolution supported by a majority of its members prior to the issue of the proclamation to which the amendment relates unless that legislative assembly, subsequently, by resolution supported by a majority of its members, revokes its dissent and authorizes the amendment.
40. Where an amendment is made under subsection 38(1) that transfers provincial legislative powers relating to education or other cultural matters from provincial legislatures to Parliament, Canada shall provide reasonable compensation to any province to which the amendment does not apply.

13 1) The office of the Queen, the Governor General and the Lieutenant Governor of a province; 2) the right of a province to a number of members in the House of Commons not less than the number of Senators by which the province was entitled to be represented in 1982; 3) the use of the English or the French language; 4) the composition of the Supreme Court of Canada and 5) an amendment of the amending formula.

In practice, a stalemate always ensues when negotiations are entered into, because this unanimity principle inevitably imposes itself. The dynamics of constitutional negotiations tend to bring about a coalescence of all the negotiating parties' demands, some of which are subject to ss. 38(1), or to s. 43, and others to s. 41. The constitutional proposals, of which the 1992 *Charlottetown Accord* is an eloquent example, become a "package deal" necessarily subject to the most stringent amending formula, that of unanimity. And because of the precedent set by the *Charlottetown Accord*, it now appears that the consent of Aboriginal and Territorial leaders, as well as a nationwide referendum would be required to enable a constitutional amendment to pass. Many reasons explain the failure of recent constitutional proposals, but the rigidity of the amending formula certainly is an important one.[14]

The division of powers will, most probably, never be amended under the present formula unless unforeseen and radical changes supervene. The gap between the wishes of the Québécois and those of the English Canadians is too

---

14 For an analysis of those reasons, see *Morin & Woehrling* 1994: 543-577. The dissatisfaction engendered by the rejection of Quebec's demands in the *Meech Lake* and *Charlottetown* accords led to the 1995 referendum where the "No" forces won the day by a only a hair's breath margin. The Supreme Court of Canada was afterwards called upon to decide whether, under Canadian constitutional law or international law, Quebec could unilaterally secede from Canada. In a very nuanced decision, although it answered no to both questions, the Court nevertheless declared that a clear vote for secession could not be ignored by the rest of Canada (*Reference Re Secession of Quebec* 1998: ¶151): "Quebec could not, despite a clear referendum result, purport to invoke a right of self-determination to dictate the terms of a proposed secession to the other parties to the federation. The democratic vote, by however strong a majority, would have no legal effect on its own and could not push aside the principles of federalism and the rule of law, the rights of individuals and minorities, or the operation of democracy in the other provinces or in Canada as a whole. Democratic rights under the Constitution cannot be divorced from constitutional obligations. Nor, however, can the reverse proposition be accepted. The continued existence and operation of the Canadian constitutional order could not be indifferent to a clear expression of a clear majority of Quebecers that they no longer wish to remain in Canada. The other provinces and the federal government would have no basis to deny the right of the government of Quebec to pursue secession, should a clear majority of the people of Quebec choose that goal, so long as in doing so, Quebec respects the rights of others. The negotiations that followed such a vote would address the potential act of secession as well as its possible terms should in fact secession proceed. There would be no conclusions predetermined by law on any issue. Negotiations would need to address the interests of the other provinces, the federal government, Quebec and indeed the rights of all Canadians both within and outside Quebec, and specifically the rights of minorities. No one suggests that it would be an easy set of negotiations."

wide. Indeed, it is interesting to note that since 1982, most proposals for constitutional reform originating from outside the province of Québec have had more to do with changes to federal institutions than with an alteration of the division of powers as it now exists. For instance, the western provinces' primary demand is for a Triple-E Senate – elected, efficient and equal.[15] In Québec, on the contrary, the emphasis has always been put on reforming the division of powers, rather than reforming the federal institutions (*Morin & Woehrling 1994: 211 footnote 251; 436-438*).

The English Canadians' attitude is hardly surprising if one accepts the fact that they consider themselves to be part of the same national community.[16] Even in the Western part of Canada, where there are stronger demands for decentralisation, these are not based on the belief, commonly held in Québec, that *inherent* provincial rights exist and that, consequently, there are areas of public policy that are federal *non grata*. From this perspective, the English Canadians' wish to reinforce the central government's powers and, at the same time, their own regional representation in Parliament is quite understandable. Centralisation is not conceived of as a threat to their national identity; on the contrary, it reinforces it. This explains why many English Canadian scholars are pleased with the centralist bent adopted by the Supreme Court of Canada.

However, this is not true for many citizens of the Québec and First Nations – i.e. aboriginal – communities. Although the majority of these citizens do feel an allegiance to Canada, they nevertheless strongly believe that they belong primarily to a different national community; one whose autonomy, in the case of Québec, is guaranteed by the barriers established by section 92 of the *Constitution Act, 1867*. Being territorially concentrated in one single province, it is no wonder that Quebecers consider their own "Parliament", the National Assembly, to be the true voice of their concerns. Centralisation, therefore, is bound to meet with their displeasure.

In other words, what opposes Québec and the rest of Canada is their different conceptions of Canadian federalism. Whereas the former envisage Canadian federalism as a "multinational federalism", that is as "a system for dividing power so as to enable meaningful [national] self-government" (*Kymlicka 1998a: 20*), the latter look upon it as a "territorial federalism", that is "a means by which a *single* national community can divide and diffuse power." (*id.: 21; my emphasis*) These different conceptions of federalism account for the im-

15 For an analysis of the many Senate reform proposals that have been made over the last four decades, see *Morin & Woehrling* 1994: 193-221.

16 The two following paragraphs borrow extensively from *Kymlicka* 1998.

possibility of modifying the Constitution in general, and the division of powers in particular. Whereas Québec wishes to be recognised as a distinct society within Canada, and claims that greater autonomy and thus more constitutional powers are necessary to its cultural development and growth, English Canada adamantly clings to the idea that all provinces should be treated equally and that no special status should be recognised to any one province. As we will now see, these different conceptions of Canadian federalism also explain the difficulty of modifying the division of powers in an *informal* manner.

II. Informal Adjustments to the Division of Powers

Even prior to 1982, amending the constitution had proved to be an extremely difficult task. Only twenty-two amendments were reached between 1867 and 1982; and just two of them, as I said earlier, had to do with the division of powers. All of these 22 amendments, with one exception that did not relate to the division of powers, were agreed to by the federal government and *all* the provinces.

Since 1982, as we have seen earlier, the obstacles to the fulfilment of constitutional reform have been compounded by the new amending formula. Québec's quest for special status and English Canada's opposition to any treatment that would clash with the formal equality of all provinces have led Canada to an impasse. For example, in trying to conciliate the "distinct society" and "equality" principles, the text of the *Charlottetown Accord* became nothing but a watered down version of these contradictory concepts. No wonder this accord was a failure in waiting. As one commentator has observed, "[r]ather than a trade-off between Quebec's demands for additional powers and western Canada's demands for a triple-E Senate, the result was a package that did not meet either demand and did not give either Quebec or the western and Atlantic provinces any reason to support it." (*McRoberts 1997: 215*).

Formally amending the constitution has thus always proved to be a difficult road to travel. As a result, informal arrangements having no foundation in either statutes, conventions of parliamentary government or in the constitution have provided the channels through which constitutional adaptation was made possible. Arrangements such as the First Ministers Conferences (annual federal-provincial conferences of the provincial Premiers and the federal Prime Minister), the Annual Premiers' Conference – and since 2003 the Council of the Federation, the Western Premiers' Conference, the Atlantic Premiers' Conference, meetings of standing federal-provincial committees of finance ministers and line ministers, have given birth to what is generally referred to as "cooperative federalism." *Peter Hogg* (*2003: 146-147*) provides the following definition:

> The essence of cooperative federalism is a network of relationships between the executives of the central and regional governments. Through these relationships mechanisms are developed, especially fiscal mechanisms, which allow a continuous redistribution of powers and resources without recourse to the courts or the amending process. These relationships are also the means by which consultations occur on the many issues of interest to both federal and provincial governments. The areas where cooperative federalism has been most dominant is in the federal-provincial financial arrangements.

As the informal arrangements enumerated above attest, "cooperative federalism" is also synonymous with "executive federalism." The latter has been described as "the predominant role of governmental executives (ministers and their officials) in intergovernmental relations in parliamentary federations where responsible first minister and cabinet ministers tend to predominate within both levels of government" (*Watts 1996: 52*).

Quite apart from the rigidity of the constitutional amendment procedure, other factors have led to the dominance of executive federalism as the primary means of adapting the constitution and more particularly, the distribution of powers. First, as we recall, the "aspect" and "double aspect" doctrines have led to an "overlap of legislation." Accordingly, both levels of government are allowed to legislate concurrently over the same matters. Negotiations are thus required to demarcate the precise extent of each order of government's legislative territory.

Secondly, executive federalism was encouraged by the fact that intrastate federalism has proven to be a failure in Canada. The Canadian Senate, whose members are appointed by the federal Prime Minister[17] on the basis of pure patronage, is "not a provincial chamber, like the German *Bundesrat*, but a partisan one" (*Pelletier 2002: 4*). The failure of the Senate to adequately represent the regions only reinforced the provincial premiers' claim that they are the only legitimate voice of their constituents. Furthermore, our British Westminster style governance, based as it is on a first-past-the-post electoral system, on a fusion of the legislative and executive powers, on party discipline and ministerial solidarity has lent support to the establishment of all-powerful

17 According to sections 24 and 32 of the *Constitution Act*, 1867, senators are appointed by the governor-general. Nevertheless, constitutional conventions require of the governor-general that he/she perform his/her duties on the advice of the Prime Minister.

executives at both the provincial and federal level.[18] Party discipline in particular makes it impossible for individual members of the political party in power in Ottawa to express the wishes and preferences of their region's constituents, if these do not meet with the approval of Cabinet. All these elements prevent Parliament (Senate and House of Commons) from performing its role as an inter-regional bargaining forum.[19] Moreover, whereas national political parties have traditionally tried to make their deputation representative of the regional, linguistic and ethnic diversity of Canada, in recent years, we have witnessed a regionalization of political parties, with the Conservative Party representing Western Canadian interests and the Bloc Québécois intent on promoting Québec's right to secede from Canada.[20] In a word, since intergovernmental relations can not take place *within* the federal institutions, they must therefore take place *between* governments (*Bakvis 2002: 7*).

The understandings brought about through the channels of executive federalism are manifested in "intergovernmental agreements" (IGA). To this day, more than a thousand such agreements have been entered into between the federal and provincial governments; the same number of interprovincial agreements are said to exist (*Poirier 2004: 427-428*). These come in a variety of forms and are thus extremely flexible tools of intergovernmental governance. However, they suffer from being negotiated behind closed doors, from contributing to "an unduly low level of citizen participation in public affairs"; finally, they also "weak[en] and dilut[e] the accountability of governments to their legislatures and to the wider public" (*Smiley 1979*) Notwithstanding these deficiencies, IGAs remain the primary means of managing intergovernmental relations.

The function of IGAs is fourfold. First, they are used to delimit the jurisdictional reach of each order of government where concurrent powers are involved. Some of these powers, such as immigration, are explicitly recognised

---

18 See *Franks* 2004 and *Morin & Woehrling* 1994: 171-2, 176 footnote 147, 178, 191-192, 224, 235-250.

19 On the diminishing role of Parliament in federal-provincial relations, see *Frank* 2004.

20 During the June 28th, 2004 elections, the Liberal Party won 135 (75 of them in Ontario) of the 308 seats in the House of Commons, the Conservative Party 99, the Bloc Québécois 54, the New Democratic Party 19, and 1 independent member was also elected. Of interest is the regional distribution of the seats. In Atlantic Canada, the Liberals won 22 seats, the Conservatives 7 and the NDP 3. In Ontario, the Liberals won 75 seats, the Conservatives 24 and the NDP 7. In Quebec, the Liberals won 21 seats and the Bloc 54. In Western Canada, the Liberals won 14 seats, the Conservatives 68, the NDP 9 and there was one lone independent in British Columbia. The Liberals also took the three seats in the Territories.

by the constitution of 1867 (s. 95). Many IGAs have been reached by the federal and Québec governments in that particular field (*Tremblay 1995: 92-93*). As mentioned earlier, the existence of a concurrent power over certain issues can also originate with the application of the "double aspect" doctrine. This issue of environmental protection is one example. This dual authority has led to the negotiation of the *1998 Canada-Wide Accord on Environmental Harmonization* (*1998 CWAEH*).

Secondly, IGAs can also serve to coordinate the exercise of exclusive federal and provincial powers that deal with closely related issues. Arrangements involving Ottawa's power over unemployment insurance and the provinces' authority over labour training is a good example. The *1995 Internal Trade Agreement* (*1995 ITA*), agreed to by the central government and all the provinces, fulfils a similar purpose. This agreement is aimed at promoting economic efficiency by removing inter-provincial barriers to the movement of products and factors of production. Since provinces have authority over intra-provincial trade and Parliament over interprovincial and international trade, their collective involvement was necessary.

Thirdly, although IGAs cannot amend the constitution, they "can modify the *exercise* of constitutional competences" (*Poirier 2004: 449*). For instance, although legislative inter-delegation, or interparliamentary delegation[21] is unconstitutional, administrative inter-delegation is not so prohibited. For example, Ottawa can delegate to a provincial administrative agency the power to regulate, according to the legal mandate it establishes, a particular federal subject-matter. IGAs have thus enabled the establishment of federal-provincial natural products marketing schemes with boards to administer them. Once concluded though, these IGAs require the enactment of legislation allowing for the administrative inter-delegation envisioned by the scheme.

Fourthly, and most importantly for our purposes, IGAs are primarily known as the "conduits for the [federal] spending power" (*Poirier 2004: 449*). Although IGAs are not a necessary prerequisite, they are usually relied upon to establish the framework according to which the spending power is to be exercised. This power has certainly been the most important lever of change to the distribution of powers since the end of the Second World War.

One must bear in mind that the fiscal power of the federal government has always far exceeded that of the provinces. In 1867, the most costly jurisdictions had been allocated to the central government: the building of interprovincial railways, roads, canals, harbours and bridges to link the provinces with each

21 I.e. the delegation of federal legislative powers to the provinces and vice versa.

other. These were necessary prerequisites to the establishment of a common market. Furthermore, the debts of all the provinces had been assumed by Ottawa. To compensate, the power to levy both direct and indirect taxes was given to the central government. Since then Ottawa has always been able to reap more revenues than it needs.

The provinces, on the other hand, were confined to direct taxation, a source of revenue seldom resorted to before the beginning of the 20th century. In 1867, no one thought that the provinces would need much revenue to operate efficiently. The Fathers of Confederation thought that the revenues generated by the public domain would be sufficient to pay for the public expenses of the provinces. Indeed, although the provinces had been allocated authority over education, health and welfare, in the *laissez-faire* context of the 1860s, these areas were not of much concern since, for the most part, they were left to the care of religious and charitable institutions. However, they have now become, by far, the most expensive jurisdictions of all, amounting today to 80% of all provincial spending (*Boadway 2004: 13*). A transfer of funds from the wealthier central government to the poorer provinces became a necessity, especially after the Second World War. This is where the federal spending power came in.

The federal spending power generally takes one of the two following forms. First, there are the unconditional transfers of funds to the provinces, better known as equalization payments. The purpose of these payments that "provinces can spend [...] according to their respective priorities," is to "[e]nsur[e] that less prosperous provinces have sufficient revenue to provide reasonably comparable levels of public services at reasonably comparable levels of taxation" (*Canada: Department of Finance*). Redistributive equity, therefore, is the basis of equalization. Being unconditional, these payments do not affect the division of powers. The same is not true though of conditional grants, better known now as "federal transfers."

These transfers are designed to support *provincial* programs in the fields of health, education and welfare so that "all Canadians receive reasonably comparable levels of public services, wherever they live" (*id.*). As of today, the most important ones are the *Canada Health Transfer* that provides provinces with support for health care; the *Canada Social Transfer* that provides support for post-secondary education, social assistance and social services; and finally, the *Health Reform Transfer* designed to support provincial health care reforms targeted to primary health care, home care and catastrophic drug coverage. These transfers are made up of a combination of tax points and cash grants.

They provide for some mandatory conditions to be met by the receiving provinces.

Before 1977, these social transfers were also referred to as "shared-cost programs" because, although usually set up unilaterally by the federal government, they were offered to the provinces as a joint venture project. The federal government would unilaterally set up the program and then, provided that provinces submitted to the conditions imposed by Ottawa, and that they were willing to bear part of the program's cost (initially 50%), the federal government would offer to provide funding. After 1977, with the introduction of *Established Programs Financing* (EPF), health care and post-secondary education were financed through "block grants." Although they remained conditional because provinces still had to spend them for certain broadly defined purposes, they were no longer related to levels of provincial spending (*Leslie 2004: 220*). After 1977, the *Canada Assistance Plan* remained the only social transfer (for social assistance and social services) where funding was split evenly between the two orders of government (except for the more well-off provinces). In 1995, it was merged with the EPF to become the *Canada Health and Social Transfer* (*Hogg 2003: 154-155; 159-160 and 161*). In 2004, the latter was subdivided into the three transfers described in the previous paragraph.

Failure to satisfy the conditions imposed by the central government results in the reduction of the cash grant to which a province is entitled. For instance, failure by a provincial health care insurance plan to satisfy the criteria of public administration, comprehensiveness, universality, portability and accessibility as they are defined by ss. 7 to 13 of the *Canada Health Act* will be sanctioned by a reduction of the cash contribution to which the province is entitled (s. 15). The same penalty will be inflicted on a province that would impose a period of minimum residency with respect to social assistance (*Federal-Provincial Fiscal Arrangements Act, ss. 24.3(1)b) and 25*).

For provinces, federal social transfers are politically impossible to refuse. Such refusal leads to double taxation of the province's citizens. The citizens of the refusing province pay federal taxes to finance a program unavailable to them, and they also pay more provincial taxes so that their own provincial government can set up a similar program.

During the 1960s and 1970s, provinces were allowed to opt out of certain federal-provincial programs, such as hospital care and social welfare. Only Québec availed itself of this opportunity. What this meant is that Québec obtained additional tax abatements. By reducing the cash grant portion of the federal transfers, this choice allowed for greater provincial autonomy.[22] Nevertheless, in 1984, the adoption of the *Canada Health Act* restored federal control by introducing the five criteria for funding enumerated above (*Pelletier 2002: 15*).

Ottawa is not about to relinquish its spending power in areas of provincial jurisdiction. Parliament's enumerated powers, however generously interpreted they might have been by the Supreme Court of Canada in recent years, are mostly concerned with specific and technical matters such as criminal law, banking, navigation and shipping, interprovincial and international trade and commerce, etc. None of these subject matters is electorally appealing. On the other hand, the spending power allows the central government to involve itself in issues that matter to the average Canadian: "Ottawa [...] seeks public credit for leadership and funding on matters that are profoundly important to all Canadians" (*Bakvis 2002: 14*). The central government has even gone so far as to completely bypass provincial governments by unilaterally introducing direct spending programs in areas of provincial authority (Millennium Scholarship Fund, Canada Research Chairs, Canada Foundation for Innovation, Medical Equipment Trust Fund, Canada Child Tax Benefit, various transfers to municipalities, etc.).

Although federal transfers certainly have been instrumental in providing Canadians with a "high minimum level of important social services" (*Hogg 2003: 160*), they have undoubtedly deeply affected the distribution of legislative powers in Canada. Under cover of its spending power, the federal government can regulate matters lying within provincial jurisdiction. As we have seen, provinces are not in a position to refuse the funds, even though they might strongly disagree with the conditions attached to them. Moreover, the IGAs that form the basis of these programs are extremely vulnerable to unilateral action on the part of the signatories. The Supreme Court has recently concluded that the principle of parliamentary sovereignty authorises Parliament to renege on a promise made to a province in an IGA. More precisely, the Court stated that Parliament could, by statute, unilaterally reduce the amount of

22 The degree of autonomy thus recognized was very limited: "[T]he 'provincial autonomy' afforded by opting-out provisions has really amounted to nothing more than a transfer of administrative responsibility to the opting-out province. It has not given that province the freedom to divert the resources, which would otherwise be committed to a federally initiated programme, into other endeavours. Federal 'compensation' to the opting-out province has been just as conditional as the federal contribution to participating provinces" (*Hogg* 2003: 163).

transfer payments it had pledged to pay to a province (*Re Canada Assistance Plan 1991*).[23]

The vulnerability of IGAs to legislative intervention makes them a poor substitute for a formal constitutional amendment. This is one of the primary reasons for Québec's opposition to any kind of political arrangements that would not be enshrined in the constitution. Another is that the latter contains no explicit provision delimiting Ottawa's spending power in fields of provincial jurisdiction.[24] The jury is still out on whether such use of the federal spending power is constitutional or not.[25] And so, Québec does not wish to recognize the legitimacy of such spending in provincial areas of jurisdiction, even if only in an informal IGA.

Québec might be right in claiming that the constitution is silent on the question of federal transfers, since ss. 16(1) of the constitution of 1982 only indirectly alludes to them. However, ss. 36(2) certainly constitutes a strong basis in favour of the constitutionality of equalization payments:

> **36.** (1) Without altering the legislative authority of Parliament or of the provincial legislatures, or the rights of any of them with respect to the exercise of their legislative authority, Parliament and the legislatures, together with the government of Canada and the provincial governments, are committed to
>
> (*a*) promoting equal opportunities for the well-being of Canadians;
>
> (*b*) furthering economic development to reduce disparity in opportunities; and
>
> (*c*) providing essential public services of reasonable quality to all Canadians.
>
> (2) Parliament and the government of Canada are committed to the principle of making equalization payments to ensure that provincial governments have suffi-

---

23 The *1992 Charlottetown Accord* established a mechanism according to which IGAs could be constitutionally protected, for a – renewable – period of five years, against unilateral legislative intervention: *Tremblay* 1995: 173-175. With the demise of the accord, these proposals never saw the light of day.

24 Attempts were made to limit the extent of the federal spending power in the defunct *1987 Meech Lake* and *1992 Charlottetown* accords. Both agreements provided for the adoption of the following provision: "106A. (1) The Government of Canada shall provide reasonable compensation to the government of a province that chooses not to participate in a national shared cost program that is established by the Government of Canada after the coming force of this section in an area of exclusive provincial jurisdiction, if the province carries on a program or initiative that is compatible with the national objectives."

25 For an overview of the arguments for and against the constitutionality of the federal spending power in areas lying within provincial jurisdiction, see Québec, *Commission on Fiscal Imbalance, Supporting document 2*, 2002. The Supreme Court, however, seems intent on casting a favourable eye upon it (*Re Canada Assistance Plan* 1991).

cient revenues to provide reasonably comparable levels of public services at reasonably comparable levels of taxation.

In 1995, the federal government introduced radical cuts to federal transfers. These were met with outrage by the provinces accusing Ottawa of downloading its deficit upon them. This led to negotiations between Ottawa and the provinces aimed at reaching a unanimous agreement on a general framework for the use of the federal spending power in areas lying within provincial authority. Unfortunately, the *1999 Social Union Framework Agreement* (*1999 SUFA*) was agreed to by the federal government and all the provinces... except Québec. Once again Canada was playing the "9-1-1 federalism" game (*Bakvis 2002: 12*)[26]. This intergovernmental agreement was designed to provide a framework according to which "[w]hen the federal government uses [...] conditional transfers, whether cost-shared or block-funded, it should proceed in a *cooperative manner* that is respectful of the provincial and territorial governments and their priorities." (*SUFA; my emphasis*). In pursuit of this objective, all *new* initiatives relating to health care, post-secondary education, social assistance and social services require the prior agreement of a majority of provincial governments.[27] It is further specified that "[a]ll provincial and territorial governments that meet or commit to meet the agreed Canada-wide objectives and agree to respect the accountability framework will receive their share of available funding." The signatories also committed themselves to establishing a dispute avoidance and resolution procedure.[28] *Pelletier* (*2002: 13*) sums up the reasons for Québec's refusal as follows:

> Quebec did not sign that agreement, seeing it as legitimizing the federal government's spending power without Ottawa offering anything tangible in return (such as a guarantee of stable funding), beyond a requirement to consult the provinces. It entrenched the federal government's role in the social sector without recognizing the primacy of provinces. Ottawa's flexibility and initiatives were preserved, while the constraints it would have to meet were fairly modest. Most important, the agreement remained silent on a major demand by Quebec: "the ability (of a province or territory) to opt out of any new or modified Canada-wide social program in areas of provincial/territorial jurisdiction with full compensation", as

26 The nine English Canadian provinces and the federal government siding together, leaving Quebec all alone. In Canada, 9-1-1 is the standard emergency phone number.

27 The six smallest provinces totalising only 14.1% of the Canadian population – the ones that stand to gain the most from federal transfers – could thus impose their will on Quebec and Ontario.

28 In April 2002, provincial and territorial governments (with the exception of Québec) accepted what has been called the Canada Health Act dispute avoidance and resolution procedure. See (CHA Dispute Avoidance and Resolution).

stipulated by the news release issued in August 1998 at the Annual Premiers' Conference in Saskatoon.

In the words of an English Canadian political scientist, "whereas the rest of Canada appears to have affirmed the legitimacy of federal intervention in areas of provincial jurisdiction by signing the agreement, Quebec once again rejected it" (*Bodnar 2004: 11*). According to the same author, this is not very surprising since the 1999 SUFA, the 1995 ITA and the 1998 CWAEH all "reaffirm, if occasionally limit, the federal government's ability to direct policy developments throughout the country" (*id.*: *10*).[29]

Québec was not against the set of social policy principles described in the Accord[30], but it was of the opinion that although provincial cooperation is necessary and inevitable, it should be done in a manner that fully respects each level of government's jurisdiction (*Pelletier 2002: 14*).

The willingness of the English Canadian provinces to accept the legitimacy of federal interventions in their fields of jurisdiction (if the price is right) is not a recent phenomenon:

> [T]here is a political cultural aspect to the decline [in jurisdictional autonomy] best illustrated by the tendency, noted as early as 1962 by James Corry[31], for the nine English speaking provinces to simply accept 'transactions with a strongly centralizing effect, increasing the leverage of the national government on the policies of provincial governments as well as on the economy of the country.' This is not to suggest that resistance to federal incursions in areas of provincial jurisdiction are absent outside Quebec, but only that such resistance does not, typically, challenge the legitimacy of such moves."[32]

---

29 SUFA even legitimises Parliament's power to unilaterally introduce direct spending programs in areas of provincial jurisdiction: "Another use of the federal spending power is making transfers to individuals and to organizations in order to promote equality of opportunity, mobility, and other Canada-wide objectives. When the federal government introduces new Canada-wide initiatives funded through direct transfers to individuals or organizations for health care, post-secondary education, social assistance and social services, it will, prior to implementation, give at least three months' notice and offer to consult. Governments participating in these consultations will have the opportunity to identify potential duplication and to propose alternative approaches to achieve flexible and effective implementation" (SUFA).

30 "Canada's social union should reflect and give expression to the fundamental values of Canadians – equality, respect for diversity, fairness, individual dignity and responsibility, and mutual aid and our responsibilities for one another" (SUFA).

31 *Corry* 1958: 103.

32 *Bodnar* 2004: 10. For a similar assessment, see *Pelletier* 2002: 13 and the authors to whom he refers.

As I said in section I, I believe that part of the reason for Québec's and the other nine provinces' respective attitudes towards the federal spending power has to do with the fundamentally different conceptions of Canadian federalism they each hold. For a majority of Quebecers, Canada is a multinational federation in which they, as members of the Québécois nation, are entitled to pledge their primary allegiance to their own local "national" government. For English Canadians, there is but one *legitimate* voice for the entire nation, and it rests with Ottawa. These different understandings of the Canadian federation and of Canadian federalism influence the way in which both Québec and the other provinces envisage the following question: which order of government should perform the most important function of the state, namely redistributive equity?

Although the federal government refuses to acknowledge it, it is fair to say that there is a fiscal imbalance in Canada. Taking that as a given, two avenues are open to rebalance the federation.[33] The first solution is the one proposed by the *Québec 2002 Commission on fiscal imbalance.* It consists of a major reallocation of tax room from the federal government to the provinces, together with a reduction of the federal transfers. From Québec's perspective, such a solution has the advantage of putting an end to federal spending in provincial areas of authority. According to the commission, under this system only equalization payments would be tolerated. For Québec, enhanced taxing power would also mean enhanced autonomy and greater accountability to its citizens. Of interest here is that, underlying this approach there is the conviction that equity is primarily a provincial and not a national responsibility. This solution challenges the federal government's claim to primary control over the redistributive function in Canada. Furthermore, although the Québec commission argues for the maintenance of a revitalized equalization program, the solution it proposes jeopardises the latter's very existence:

> Maintenance of an effective equalization program was a key part of the Seguin (sic) Commission's recommendations. [...] The decentralization of revenue-raising responsibility to the provinces makes it more difficult for the federal government to fulfil this mandate. It both increases the degree of disparities among the provinces and reduces the revenues available for the federal government to finance equalization. Perhaps as important, it might make it more difficult to maintain the political and societal consensus required to sustain an effective equalization program. (*Boadway 2004: 11-12*).

A second avenue is open: one that would provide a solution to the fiscal imbalance without compromising the federal government's redistributive function. It consists in maintaining the federal share of the tax room and in increas-

---

33 Ideas in the following two paragraphs are extensively borrowed from *Boadway* 2004.

ing the amount of federal transfers to the provinces. In doing so, this option would preserve the existing tax harmonisation[34] that makes the maintenance of some national standards of redistributive equity possible. This would also prevent the tax competition to which the more decentralised taxing system proposed by the Québec commission would inevitably lead. Finally, and most importantly, such an approach is founded on a conviction that redistribution is, at least in some measure, national in nature[35], and that the federal spending power in matters of provincial concern is legitimate because it "is arguably the only effective policy instrument available for the federal government to fulfil [its redistributive] commitments" (*id.: 11*). In the words of *Peter Hogg*, cash grants "[are vital to a continuing federal influence over health and social assistance, because it is the power to withhold all or part of the grant which is the sanction against non-compliance by a province with federal conditions" (*2003: 155; see also 159-160*).

In other words, the Québec commission's solution is problematic for English Canadians who share a "territorial" understanding of Canadian federalism, because "[t]urning over tax room to the provinces essentially reduces the ability of the federal government to use transfers to achieve national objectives, and possibly jeopardizes the efficiency associated with a harmonized tax system" (*Boadway 2004: 12*).[36]

---

34 This harmonization has slowly dwindled in recent years: "There is no question that Canada now has a more diverse system of income taxes, personal and corporate, than was the case a few years ago" (*Leslie*: 225; see also 224-226).

35 I personally believe that a great number of Quebecers would agree with this assumption. A 2001 pole referred to by *Cutler* and *Mendelsohn* confirmed that, even though there was much less enthusiasm in Quebec for cooperative federalism, most Quebecers preferred this model of federalism over a more compartmentalized approach (2005: 84).

36 Public opinion polls seem to confirm English Canadians' acceptance of Ottawa's involvement in provincial affairs. At the end of an empirical study based on surveys and interviews, *Fred Cutler* and *Matthew Mendelsohn* came to the following conclusion (2005: 86): "Our data suggest that in the context of competitive state building and the constitutional authority of provincial governments over many areas of social life, the federal government has lost many battles but won the war. During times of intense intergovernmental conflict, public opinion does seem to coalesce around provincial grievances. But in the long run, it appears that citizens have come to value the steadying hand, and perhaps purse, of the federal government. Outside of Quebec, they support no retrenchment of the federal role in national programs and national life. If one construes the province-building argument as stressing a *shift* in support *from* the federal *to* the provincial one – as if citizens conceive of their support of multiple orders of government as zero sum – then we are confident in rejecting it. Al-

III. Conclusion

For Canadian federalism to evolve, be it through formal amendments or informal procedures, one solution[37] might be to introduce the concept of asymmetry as a means of reconciling the relationship between Québec and the rest of Canada. The very recent September 2004 *Health Care Agreement* reached by the federal government and all the provinces might be a sign that times are changing. Indeed, after enumerating the principles upon which all the premiers had agreed, the official communiqué reads as follows (*10-Year Plan to Strengthen Health Care*):

> Recognizing that an asymmetrical federalism allows for the existence of specific agreements for any province, First Ministers also agreed that a separate communiqué be released to reflect the arrangements between the Government of Canada and the Government of Québec regarding the interpretation and the implementation of the present communiqué. The funding provided by the federal government will be used by the government of Québec to implement its own plan aiming, notably, at ensuring access to quality care in a timely manner and at reducing waiting times.

As for the separate communiqué (*Asymmetric Federalism that Respects Quebec's Jurisdiction*), it states that:

> Recognizing the Government of Quebec's desire to exercise its own responsibilities with respect to planning, organizing and managing health services within its territory, and noting that its commitment with regard to the underlying principles of its public health system – universality, portability, comprehensiveness, accessibility and public administration – coincides with that of all governments in Canada, and resting on asymmetrical federalism, that is, flexible federalism that notably allows for the existence of specific agreements and arrangements adapted

---

though the division of powers may have structured some of the conflict and competition within Canadian societies, it has produced few Canadians who have any attachment to the division of powers as laid out the constitution. If there has been a neoinstitutional effect of institutions on citizens in these areas, it is through the less formal institutions of the spending power and national standards: Canadians now see the federal government as an indispensable partner even in social policies that are the section 92 preserve of the provinces. Federal action in these areas since the Second Word War has conditioned Canadians to support that involvement. Calls for a return to a classical model of federalism miss the point of what has happened over the twentieth century: Canadians support a practice of federalism where both governments are involved in most things, as governments have been for the adult lives of just about every Canadian."

37 Another might be to reinforce the role of legislatures and of the wider public in the Canadian intergovernmental system. For reform proposals of this nature that would not entail formal constitutional amendments, see *Franks* 2004 and *Cameron* 2004.

> to Quebec's specificity, the Prime Minister of Canada and the Premier of Quebec have agreed that Quebec's support for the joint communiqué following the federal-provincial-territorial first ministers' meeting is to be interpreted and implemented as follows:

Whether this will prove to be a radical change of attitude on the part of Ottawa and the nine English Canadian provinces or simply an exception that confirms the rule, is yet to be seen.

One thing is certain though: whether federal and provincial politicians achieve formal constitutional reforms or informal modifications by means of IGAs, courts will continue to incrementally adapt the division of powers along the lines that they choose to follow.

References

Statutes

Canada Health Act, R.S.C. 1985, c. C-6: http://www.hc-sc.gc.ca/medicare/Canada%20Health%20Act.htm.

Constitution Act, 1867 (U.K.), 30 & 31 Vict. c. 3: http://laws.justice.gc.ca/en/const/c1867_e.html#pre.

Constitution Act, 1982, Schedule B to the Canada Act 1982, (U.K.) 1982, c. 11: http://laws.justice.gc.ca/en/const/annex_e.html#I.

Federal-Provincial Fiscal Arrangements Act, R.S.C. 1985, c. F-8: http://laws.justice.gc.ca/en/F-8/58332.html.

Statute of Westminster, 22 George V, c. 4 (U.K.): http://www.solon.org/Constitutions/Canada/English/StatuteofWestminster.html.

Books and Periodicals

Bakvis, Herman and Grace Skogstad. 2002. "Canadian Federalism: Performance, Effectiveness, and Legitimacy." In: Canadian Federalism: Performance, Effectiveness, and Legitimacy, ed. *Bakvis, Herman and Grace Skogstad*, Don Mills, Oxford University Press: 3-23.

Boadway, Robin. 2004. "Should the Canadian Federation be Rebalanced?", working-paper #2004-1, Economic Policy Research Institute Working Paper Series, University of Western Ontario: http://www.ssc.uwo.ca/economics/centers/epri/wp2004/Boadway01.pdf.

Bodnar, Cameron D. 2004. "Reconciling the Irreconcilable: A Theoretical Take on the Prospects for Intergovernmental Peace in Canada", paper prepared for the 2004 Annual Meeting of the Canadian Political Science Association, Winnipeg: http://www.cpsa-acsp.ca/papers-2004/Bodnar.pdf.

Cairns, Alan C. 1971. "The Judicial Committee and Its Critics", Canadian Journal of Political Science, vol. 30: 301-345.

Cameron, David. 2004. "Inter-Legislative Federalism." In: Canada: The State of the Federation 2002 – Reconsidering the Institutions of Canadian Federalism, ed. *J. Peter Meekison, Hamish Telford and Harvey Lazar*, Kingston: Institute of Intergovernmental Relations, Queen's University: 463-482.

Corry, James. 1958. "Constitutional Trends and Federalism." In: eds. *A.R.M., F.R. Scott, and al.*, Evolving Canadian Federalism. – Durham, N.C.: Duke University Press: 92-125.

Courchene, Thomas J. 2004. "Pan-Canadian Provincialism – The New Federalism and the Old Constitution", Options politiques/Policy Options November Issue: 20-28.

Cutler, Fred and Matthew Mendelsohn. 2005. "Unnatural loyalties or Naive Collaborationalists: The Governments and Citizens of Canadian Federalism". In: Insiders & Outsiders – Alan Cairns and the Reshaping of Canadian Citizenship, eds. *Gerald Kernerman and Philip Resnick*, University of British Columbia Press: 71-89.

Franks, C.E.S. 2004. "A Continuing Canadian Conundrum: The Role of Parliament in Questions of National Unity and the Processes of Amending the Constitution." In: Canada: The State of the Federation 2002 – Reconsidering the Institutions of Canadian Federalism, eds. *J. Peter Meekison, Hamish Telford and Harvey Lazar*, Kingston: Institute of Intergovernmental Relations, Queen's University: 35-55.

Gibbins, Roger. 2001. "Shifting Sands: Exploring the Political Foundations of SUFA", Policy Matters/Enjeux publics, July issue, vol. 2, no. 3: http://www.irpp.org/pm/archive/pmvol2no3.pdf.

Hogg, Peter W. 2003. Constitutional Law of Canada, Toronto: Student Edition, Thomson/Carswell.

And *Wade K. Wright.* 2004. "Canadian Federalism, the Privy Council and the Supreme Court: Reflections on the Debate About Canadian Federalism", University of British Columbia Law Review forthcoming.

2005. "The Legacy of the Privy Council in Canadian Federalism" In: Insiders & Outsiders – Alan Cairns and the Reshaping of Canadian Citizenship, eds. *Gerald Kernerman and Philip Resnick,* University of British Columbia Press: 65-70.

Kymlicka, Will. 1998. Finding Our Way – Rethinking Ethnocultural Relations in Canada, Don Mills: Oxford University Press.

1998a. "Multinational Federalism in Canada: Rethinking the Partnership." In: Beyond the Impasse: Toward Reconciliation, eds. *Roger Gibbins and Guy LaForest,* Montreal: Institute for Research on Public Policy: 15-50.

Leclair, Jean. 1993. "Droit constitutionnel – Partage des compétences – Loi réglementant les produits du tabac, L.C. 1988, c. 20 – La théorie des dimensions nationales: une boîte à phantasmes: Canada (Procureur Général) c. R.J.R. – MacDonald Inc.", Canadian Bar Review, vol. 72, at 524-538.

2003. "The Supreme Court's Understanding of Federalism: Efficiency at the Expense of Diversity", Queen's Law Journal, vol. 28, at 411-454.

2004. "The Elusive Quest for the Quintessential 'National Interest" University of British Columbia Law Review forthcoming.

Leslie, Peter, Ronald H. Neumann and Russ Robinson. 2004. "Managing Canadian Fiscal Federalism." In: Canada: The State of the Federation 2002 – Reconsidering the Institutions of Canadian Federalism, eds. *J. Peter Meekison, Hamish Telford and Harvey Lazar*, Kingston, Institute of Intergovernmental Relations, Queen's University: 213-248.

McRoberts, Kenneth. 1997. Misconceiving Canada – The Struggle for National Unity. Toronto: Oxford University Press.

Morin, Jacques-Yvan, and José Woehrling. 1994. Les Constitutions du Canada et du Québec du régime français à nos jours. Montréal: Les Éditions Thémis.

Pelletier, Réjean. 2002. "Intergovernmental Cooperation Mechanisms: Factors for Change?" In: Commission on the Future of Health Care in Canada; discussion paper no. 29: http://www.hc-sc.gc.ca/english/pdf/romanow/pdfs/29_Pelletier_E.pdf.

Poirier, Johanne. 2004. "Intergovernmental Agreements in Canada: At the Crossroads Between Law and Politics." In: Canada: The State of the Federation 2002 – Reconsidering the Institutions of Canadian Federalism, eds. *J. Peter Meekison, Hamish Telford and Harvey Lazar*, Kingston: Institute of Intergovernmental Relations, Queen's University: 425-462.

Smiley, Donald. 1979. "An Outsider's Observations of Intergovernmental Relations Among Consenting Adults." In: Confrontation or Collaboration: Intergovernmental in Canada Today, ed. *Richard Simeon,* Montreal: Institute for Research on Public Policy, at 105-113.

Tremblay, André. 1995. La réforme de la constitution au Canada. Montréal: Les Éditions Thémis.

Watts, Ronald L. 1996. Comparing Federalism in the 1990s. Kingston: Institute of Intergovernmental Relations, Queen's University.

Case law

Bell Canada v. Québec (CSST), [1988] 1 R.C.S. 749.

General Motors v. City National Leasing, [1989] 1 R.C.S. 641.

Re Canada Assistance Plan, [1991] 2 S.C.R. 525.

R. v. Crown Zellerbach Canada Ltd., [1988] 1 S.C.R. 401.

Re Resolution to amend the Constitution, [1981] 1 S.C.R. 753.

Reference re Objection by Quebec to a Resolution to Amend the Constitution, [1982] 2 S.C.R. 793.

Reference re Secession of Quebec, [1998] 2 S.C.R. 217.

Governmental Documents

10-year Plan to Strengthen Health Care: http://pm.gc.ca/eng/news.asp?id=260.

Asymmetric Federalism that Respects Quebec's Jurisdiction: http://pm.gc.ca/grfx/docs/QuebecENG.pdf.

Canada-Wide Accord on Environmental Harmonization (1998): http://www.ccme.ca/assets/pdf/cws_accord_env_harmonization.pdf.

CHA Dispute Avoidance and Resolution (2002): http://www.hc-sc.gc.ca/english/media/releases/2002/health_act/cha.htm.

Internal Trade Agreement (1995): http://www.cse.gov.bc.ca/ProgramsAndServices/Trade/AIT.htm.

Québec. Commission on Fiscal Imbalance (2002). A New Division of Canada's Financial Resources. Report: http://www.desequilibrefiscal.gouv.qc.ca/en/document/rapport_final.htm.

Québec. Commission on Fiscal Imbalance (2002). The "Federal Spending Power". Report. Supporting Document 2: http://www.desequilibrefiscal.gouv.qc.ca/en/document/pouvoir.htm.

Social Union Framework Agreement (1999): http://socialunion.gc.ca/news/020499_e.html.

Transfer Payments to Provinces, Canada, Department of Finance: http://www.fin.gc.ca/FEDPROV/eqpe.html.

Annex A

CONSTITUTION ACT, 1867

VI. DISTRIBUTION OF LEGISLATIVE POWERS

POWERS OF THE PARLIAMENT

Legislative Authority of Parliament of Canada

91. It shall be lawful for the Queen, by and with the Advice and Consent of the Senate and House of Commons, to make Laws for the Peace, Order, and good Government of Canada, in relation to all Matters not coming within the Classes of Subjects by this Act assigned exclusively to the Legislatures of the Provinces; and for greater Certainty, but not so as to restrict the Generality of the foregoing Terms of this Section, it is hereby declared that (notwithstanding anything in this Act) the exclusive Legislative Authority of the Parliament of Canada extends to all Matters coming within the Classes of Subjects next hereinafter enumerated; that is to say,

1. Repealed.
1A. The Public Debt and Property.
2. The Regulation of Trade and Commerce.
2A. Unemployment insurance.
3. The raising of Money by any Mode or System of Taxation.
4. The borrowing of Money on the Public Credit.
5. Postal Service.
6. The Census and Statistics.
7. Militia, Military and Naval Service, and Defence.
8. The fixing of and providing for the Salaries and Allowances of Civil and other Officers of the Government of Canada.
9. Beacons, Buoys, Lighthouses, and Sable Island.
10. Navigation and Shipping.
11. Quarantine and the Establishment and Maintenance of Marine Hospitals.

12. Sea Coast and Inland Fisheries.
13. Ferries between a Province and any British or Foreign Country or between Two Provinces.
14. Currency and Coinage.
15. Banking, Incorporation of Banks, and the Issue of Paper Money.
16. Savings Banks.
17. Weights and Measures.
18. Bills of Exchange and Promissory Notes.
19. Interest.
20. Legal Tender.
21. Bankruptcy and Insolvency.
22. Patents of Invention and Discovery.
23. Copyrights.
24. Indians and Lands reserved for the Indians.
25. Naturalization and Aliens.
26. Marriage and Divorce.
27. The Criminal Law, except the Constitution of Courts of Criminal Jurisdiction, but including the Procedure in Criminal Matters.
28. The Establishment, Maintenance, and Management of Penitentiaries.
29. Such Classes of Subjects as are expressly excepted in the Enumeration of the Classes of Subjects by this Act assigned exclusively to the Legislatures of the Provinces.

And any Matter coming within any of the Classes of Subjects enumerated in this Section shall not be deemed to come within the Class of Matters of a local or private Nature comprised in the Enumeration of the Classes of Subjects by this Act assigned exclusively to the Legislatures of the Provinces.

EXCLUSIVE POWERS OF PROVINCIAL LEGISLATURES

Subjects of exclusive Provincial Legislation

92. In each Province the Legislature may exclusively make Laws in relation to Matters coming within the Classes of Subjects next hereinafter enumerated; that is to say,

1. Repealed.
2. Direct Taxation within the Province in order to the raising of a Revenue for Provincial Purposes.
3. The borrowing of Money on the sole Credit of the Province.
4. The Establishment and Tenure of Provincial Offices and the Appointment and Payment of Provincial Officers.
5. The Management and Sale of the Public Lands belonging to the Province and of the Timber and Wood thereon.
6. The Establishment, Maintenance, and Management of Public and Reformatory Prisons in and for the Province.
7. The Establishment, Maintenance, and Management of Hospitals, Asylums, Charities, and Eleemosynary Institutions in and for the Province, other than Marine Hospitals.
8. Municipal Institutions in the Province.
9. Shop, Saloon, Tavern, Auctioneer, and other Licences in order to the raising of a Revenue for Provincial, Local, or Municipal Purposes.
10. Local Works and Undertakings other than such as are of the following Classes:
    (a) Lines of Steam or other Ships, Railways, Canals, Telegraphs, and other Works and Undertakings connecting the Province with any other or others of the Provinces, or extending beyond the Limits of the Province:
    (b) Lines of Steam Ships between the Province and any British or Foreign Country:
    (c) Such Works as, although wholly situate within the Province, are before or after their Execution declared by the Parliament of Canada to be for the general Advantage of Canada or for the Advantage of Two or more of the Provinces.
11. The Incorporation of Companies with Provincial Objects.
12. The Solemnization of Marriage in the Province.
13. Property and Civil Rights in the Province.
14. The Administration of Justice in the Province, including the Constitution, Maintenance, and Organization of Provincial Courts, both of Civil and of Criminal Jurisdiction, and including Procedure in Civil Matters in those Courts.

15. The Imposition of Punishment by Fine, Penalty, or Imprisonment for enforcing any Law of the Province made in relation to any Matter coming within any of the Classes of Subjects enumerated in this Section.
16. Generally all Matters of a merely local or private Nature in the Province.

NON-RENEWABLE NATURAL RESOURCES, FORESTRY RESOURCES AND ELECTRICAL ENERGY

Laws respecting non-renewable natural resources, forestry resources and electrical energy

92A. (1) In each province, the legislature may exclusively make laws in relation to

(a) exploration for non-renewable natural resources in the province;

(b) development, conservation and management of non-renewable natural resources and forestry resources in the province, including laws in relation to the rate of primary production therefrom; and

(c) development, conservation and management of sites and facilities in the province for the generation and production of electrical energy.

Export from provinces of resources

(2) In each province, the legislature may make laws in relation to the export from the province to another part of Canada of the primary production from non-renewable natural resources and forestry resources in the province and the production from facilities in the province for the generation of electrical energy, but such laws may not authorize or provide for discrimination in prices or in supplies exported to another part of Canada.

Authority of Parliament

(3) Nothing in subsection (2) derogates from the authority of Parliament to enact laws in relation to the matters referred to in that subsection and, where such a law of Parliament and a law of a province conflict, the law of Parliament prevails to the extent of the conflict.

Taxation of resources

(4) In each province, the legislature may make laws in relation to the raising of money by any mode or system of taxation in respect of

(a) non-renewable natural resources and forestry resources in the province and the primary production therefrom, and

(b) sites and facilities in the province for the generation of electrical energy and the production therefrom,

whether or not such production is exported in whole or in part from the province, but such laws may not authorize or provide for taxation that differentiates between production exported to another part of Canada and production not exported from the province.

"Primary production"

(5) The expression "primary production" has the meaning assigned by the Sixth Schedule.

Existing powers or rights

(6) Nothing in subsections (1) to (5) derogates from any powers or rights that a legislature or government of a province had immediately before the coming into force of this section.

EDUCATION

Legislation respecting Education

93. In and for each Province the Legislature may exclusively make Laws in relation to Education, subject and according to the following Provisions:

(1) Nothing in any such Law shall prejudicially affect any Right or Privilege with respect to Denominational Schools which any Class of Persons have by Law in the Province at the Union:

(2) All the Powers, Privileges, and Duties at the Union by Law conferred and imposed in Upper Canada on the Separate Schools and School Trustees of the Queen's Roman Catholic Subjects shall be and the same are hereby extended to the Dissentient Schools of the Queen's Protestant and Roman Catholic Subjects in Quebec:

(3) Where in any Province a System of Separate or Dissentient Schools exists by Law at the Union or is thereafter established by the Legislature of the Province, an Appeal shall lie to the Governor General in Council from any Act or Decision of any Provincial Authority affecting any Right or Privilege of the Protestant or Roman Catholic Minority of the Queen's Subjects in relation to Education:

(4) In case any such Provincial Law as from Time to Time seems to the Governor General in Council requisite for the due Execution of the Provisions of this Section is not made, or in case any Decision of the Governor General in Council on any Appeal under this Section is not duly executed by the proper Provincial Authority in that Behalf, then and in every such Case, and as far only as the Circumstances of each Case require, the Parliament of Canada may make remedial Laws for the due Execution of the Provisions of this Section and of any Decision of the Governor General in Council under this Section.

93A. Paragraphs (1) to (4) of section 93 do not apply to Quebec.

UNIFORMITY OF LAWS IN ONTARIO, NOVA SCOTIA, AND NEW BRUNSWICK

Legislation for Uniformity of Laws in Three Provinces

94. Notwithstanding anything in this Act, the Parliament of Canada may make Provision for the Uniformity of all or any of the Laws relative to Property and Civil Rights in Ontario, Nova Scotia, and New Brunswick, and of the Procedure of all or any of the Courts in those Three Provinces, and from and after the passing of any Act in that Behalf the Power of the Parliament of Canada to make Laws in relation to any Matter comprised in any such Act shall, notwithstanding anything in this Act, be unrestricted; but any Act of the Parliament of Canada making Provision for such Uniformity shall not have effect in any Province unless and until it is adopted and enacted as Law by the Legislature thereof.

OLD AGE PENSIONS

Legislation respecting old age pensions and supplementary benefits

94A. The Parliament of Canada may make laws in relation to old age pensions and supplementary benefits, including survivors' and disability benefits irrespective of age, but no such law shall affect the operation of any law present or future of a provincial legislature in relation to any such matter.

AGRICULTURE AND IMMIGRATION

Concurrent Powers of Legislation respecting Agriculture, etc.

95. In each Province the Legislature may make Laws in relation to Agriculture in the Province, and to Immigration into the Province; and it is hereby declared that the Parliament of Canada may from Time to Time make Laws in relation to Agriculture in all or any of the Provinces, and to Immigration into all or any of the Provinces; and any Law of the Legislature of a Province relative to Agriculture or to Immigration shall have effect in and for the Province as long and as far only as it is not repugnant to any Act of the Parliament of Canada.

Transfer of Property in Schedule

108. The Public Works and Property of each Province, enumerated in the Third Schedule to this Act, shall be the Property of Canada.

Property in Lands, Mines, etc.

109. All Lands, Mines, Minerals, and Royalties belonging to the several Provinces of Canada, Nova Scotia, and New Brunswick at the Union, and all Sums then due or payable for such Lands, Mines, Minerals, or Royalties, shall belong to the several Provinces of Ontario, Quebec, Nova Scotia, and New Brunswick in which the same are situate or arise, subject to any Trusts existing in respect thereof, and to any Interest other than that of the Province in the same.

Canada to be liable for Provincial Debts

111. Canada shall be liable for the Debts and Liabilities of each Province existing at the Union.

Canadian Manufactures, etc.

121. All Articles of the Growth, Produce, or Manufacture of any one of the Provinces shall, from and after the Union, be admitted free into each of the other Provinces.

Annex B

CONSTITUTION ACT, 1982

PART III

EQUALIZATION AND REGIONAL DISPARITIES

Commitment to promote equal opportunities

36. (1) Without altering the legislative authority of Parliament or of the provincial legislatures, or the rights of any of them with respect to the exercise of their legislative authority, Parliament and the legislatures, together with the government of Canada and the provincial governments, are committed to

(*a*) promoting equal opportunities for the well-being of Canadians;

(*b*) furthering economic development to reduce disparity in opportunities; and

(*c*) providing essential public services of reasonable quality to all Canadians.

Commitment respecting public services

(2) Parliament and the government of Canada are committed to the principle of making equalization payments to ensure that provincial governments have sufficient revenues to provide reasonably comparable levels of public services at reasonably comparable levels of taxation.

PART V

PROCEDURE FOR AMENDING CONSTITUTION OF CANADA

General procedure for amending Constitution of Canada

38. (1) An amendment to the Constitution of Canada may be made by proclamation issued by the Governor General under the Great Seal of Canada where so authorized by

(*a*) resolutions of the Senate and House of Commons; and
(*b*) resolutions of the legislative assemblies of at least two-thirds of the provinces that have, in the aggregate, according to the then latest general census, at least fifty per cent of the population of all the provinces.

Majority of members

(2) An amendment made under subsection (1) that derogates from the legislative powers, the proprietary rights or any other rights or privileges of the legislature or government of a province shall require a resolution supported by a majority of the members of each of the Senate, the House of Commons and the legislative assemblies required under subsection (1).

Expression of dissent

(3) An amendment referred to in subsection (2) shall not have effect in a province the legislative assembly of which has expressed its dissent thereto by resolution supported by a majority of its members prior to the issue of the proclamation to which the amendment relates unless that legislative assembly, subsequently, by resolution supported by a majority of its members, revokes its dissent and authorizes the amendment.

Revocation of dissent

(4) A resolution of dissent made for the purposes of subsection (3) may be revoked at any time before or after the issue of the proclamation to which it relates.

Restriction on proclamation

39. (1) A proclamation shall not be issued under subsection 38(1) before the expiration of one year from the adoption of the resolution initiating the amendment procedure thereunder, unless the legislative assembly of each province has previously adopted a resolution of assent or dissent.

Idem

(2) A proclamation shall not be issued under subsection 38(1) after the expiration of three years from the adoption of the resolution initiating the amendment procedure thereunder.

Compensation

40. Where an amendment is made under subsection 38(1) that transfers provincial legislative powers relating to education or other cultural matters from provincial legislatures to Parliament, Canada shall provide reasonable compensation to any province to which the amendment does not apply.

Amendment by unanimous consent

41. An amendment to the Constitution of Canada in relation to the following matters may be made by proclamation issued by the Governor General under the Great Seal of Canada only where authorized by resolutions of the Senate and House of Commons and of the legislative assembly of each province:

(*a*) the office of the Queen, the Governor General and the Lieutenant Governor of a province;

(*b*) the right of a province to a number of members in the House of Commons not less than the number of Senators by which the province is entitled to be represented at the time this Part comes into force;

(*c*) subject to section 43, the use of the English or the French language;

(*d*) the composition of the Supreme Court of Canada; and

(*e*) an amendment to this Part.

Amendment by general procedure

42. (1) An amendment to the Constitution of Canada in relation to the following matters may be made only in accordance with subsection 38(1):

(*a*) the principle of proportionate representation of the provinces in the House of Commons prescribed by the Constitution of Canada;

(*b*) the powers of the Senate and the method of selecting Senators;

(*c*) the number of members by which a province is entitled to be represented in the Senate and the residence qualifications of Senators;

(*d*) subject to paragraph 41(*d*), the Supreme Court of Canada;

(*e*) the extension of existing provinces into the territories; and (*f*) notwithstanding any other law or practice, the establishment of new provinces.

Exception (2) Subsections 38(2) to (4) do not apply in respect of amendments in relation to matters referred to in subsection (1).

Amendment of provisions relating to some but not all provinces

43. An amendment to the Constitution of Canada in relation to any provision that applies to one or more, but not all, provinces, including

(*a*) any alteration to boundaries between provinces, and

(*b*) any amendment to any provision that relates to the use of the English or the French language within a province,

may be made by proclamation issued by the Governor General under the Great Seal of Canada only where so authorized by resolutions of the Senate and House of Commons and of the legislative assembly of each province to which the amendment applies.

Amendments by Parliament

44. Subject to sections 41 and 42, Parliament may exclusively make laws amending the Constitution of Canada in relation to the executive government of Canada or the Senate and House of Commons.

Amendments by provincial legislatures

45. Subject to section 41, the legislature of each province may exclusively make laws amending the constitution of the province.

Initiation of amendment procedures

46. (1) The procedures for amendment under sections 38, 41, 42 and 43 may be initiated either by the Senate or the House of Commons or by the legislative assembly of a province.

Revocation of authorization

(2) A resolution of assent made for the purposes of this Part may be revoked at any time before the issue of a proclamation authorized by it.

Amendments without Senate resolution

47. (1) An amendment to the Constitution of Canada made by proclamation under section 38, 41, 42 or 43 may be made without a resolution of the Senate authorizing the issue of the proclamation if, within one hundred and eighty days after the adoption by the House of Commons of a resolution authorizing its issue, the Senate has not adopted such a resolution and if, at any time after the expiration of that period, the House of Commons again adopts the resolution.

Computation of period

(2) Any period when Parliament is prorogued or dissolved shall not be counted in computing the one hundred and eighty day period referred to in subsection (1).

Advice to issue proclamation

48. The Queen's Privy Council for Canada shall advise the Governor General to issue a proclamation under this Part forthwith on the adoption of the resolutions required for an amendment made by proclamation under this Part.

Constitutional conference

49. A constitutional conference composed of the Prime Minister of Canada and the first ministers of the provinces shall be convened by the Prime Minister of Canada within fifteen years after this Part comes into force to review the provisions of this Part.

ELISEO AJA

THE DEBATE ABOUT COMPETENCIES IN SPAIN*

Spain is an old state but has a short experience in democracy, reduced to the 25 years since the approval of the current 1978 constitution. The most part of our history has been dominated by authoritarian governments, which were also very centralistic. The short experience of the Second Republic (1931-36) was a precedent of democracy and decentralisation but was followed by 40 years of General Franco's dictatorship, the most authoritarian and centralist government of all eras. In the new democracy the constitution had to answer petitions of autonomy, especially in Catalonia and Basque Country. In the 25 years of the constitution we have built a serious regime of human rights, a modern monarchy, a parliamentarian system with a strong chancellor, an ambitious Constitutional Court and a large territorial self-government. All these institutions consolidated, except for the last one, the territorial organisation of power in Autonomous Communities (AACC).

Why? The answer must be complex. One cause could be the defects in the distribution of power, but also the deficiencies in the relationship among the AACC and with the state. But we must consider moreover the significant political factor, like the existence of two big general parties (conservative –called popular party – and socialist) along with the several nationalistic parties of Catalonia, Basque Country, Galicia, Canary Island and others. These parties are very important factors in the institutions of its Autonomous Community (AC) but also in the Spanish Parliament, operating as a hinge to form a parliamentary majority. So the reflection on the competencies in Spain must not forget the more general problems of autonomy, even the general structure of the state.

Also, the social reality is complex. Spain has 42 million people, and the state is divided into 17 Autonomous Communities and more than 9,000 municipalities. Some are big cities (Madrid, Barcelona, Bilbao, Sevilla, etc.) but most of them are very small. Also, the AACC are too diverse, from the small La Rioja to the biggest Andalusia, from the historical Catalonia to the new entity of Murcia or Extremadura, and some people think that the autonomous state has been badly built.

---

* The main bibliography and constitutional judgments can be found in my book *El Estado autonómico. Federalismo y hechos diferenciales*, (The autonomous State. Federalism and differential facts), Madrid, 1999, Alianza (2ª ed., 2003).

GRAPH 1: AUTONOMOUS COMMUNITIES AND INHABITANTS

AACC	Population
Andalucía	7.478.432
Aragón	1.217.514
Asturias	1.073.971
Islas Baleares	916.968
Canarias	1.843.755
Cantabria	542.275
Castilla y León	2.480.369
Castilla-La Mancha	1.782.038
Cataluña	6.506.440
Comunidad Valenciana	4.326.708
Extremadura	1.073.050
Galicia	2.737.370
Madrid	5.527.152
Murcia	1.226.993
Navarra	569.628
País Vasco	2.108.281
La Rioja	281.614
Total Spain	41.692.558

I. General Trends of an Autonomous State

The subtitle of my last book on the character of the Spanish autonomous state is "Federalism and Differential Fact", and I try to explain that the autonomous state is the sum of two different axes: on the one hand, the structure and running of the institutions which are equivalent to the European federal systems, and on the other hand, the powers and specific dynamics of some territorial entities – like Basque Country or Catalonia – with different languages, civil law and their own police, etc., elements which we know as the "differential fact" or "differential factors." Decision making in this kind of compound state is more difficult and needs specific procedures, unknown in classical federalism. Moreover, one must remember the existence of several nationalist parties in these AACC, with representation also in the central parliament.

The constitution of Spain avoids all traditional terms of federalism. The central power is called state, the territorial entities are denominated Autonomous Communities, and, in fact, people think that our system is not a federal one, and there is not a clear idea about which kind of state it is. In any case, this change to the autonomous state could be described as a major upheaval: until 1978 Spain was the most centralist state in Europe and now has become one of the most decentralized ones. The AACC account for approximately 50% of all the country's civil servants (the rest is divided between central and local administration). However, it is not merely a question of administrative decentralization, because the AACC have important legislative power in different spheres.

The first axis of autonomous state presents some elements that correspond to the nature of the central European federalism, halfway between Germany and Austria. We can review the main characteristics of the Spanish system in comparison with the traditional components of a federal type of state.

1. The constitutional rank of autonomy

The autonomy has a constitutional rank recognized formally by the constitution, and also every AC – like every Land – has its own constitution, called *Statute of Autonomy*, that acts as the supreme law of the territory. However, unlike in the majority of federal systems, the elaboration and reform requires the joint intervention of AC and state with qualified majorities.

2. Constitutional distribution of competencies

The division of powers between the state and the AACC also has constitutional guarantee, to avoid being changed by one concrete Act, and the Constitutional Court solves conflicts concerning the respective power over one subject pursuant to legal criteria. Really, the concrete degree of the competences of every Autonomous Community derives together from the Constitution and the Statute of Autonomy of the Community. One of the most important advantages of the Constitutional Court system rests upon the general value of constitutional sentences, making the interpretation of the different categories of competencies easier.

3. The institutions of self-government of every AC

The institutional organization of every AC consists of parliament, president and government, and they depend only on democratic elections. There is no kind of hierarchical relationship with the central government. Obviously that means that the political orientation of the central and state majority can be different, and certainly we have an outstanding political pluralism. (The existence of territorial division in the judicial power is more complicated and problematic, and it will probably be reformed).

4. The financing of the states following objective criteria

Like the majority of financial systems the Spanish one is mixed, with own taxes of the AACC and others shared with the state. It has been reformed several times, and it is also under a general idea of reform. The particularity lies in the different income system of Basque Country and Navarra.

5. The procedures of relationship between the states and the AACC

The procedures of relationship between the states and the AACC are less developed than in other European federal systems, partially because the constitution did not foresee them, partially because we have difficulties to incorporate the new tools of cooperative federalism, partially also because the dynamic of nationalist parties in autonomic government prefers to maintain a relationship only with the central government. We call that "bilateralism." The creation of the Autonomous Presidents Conference only in the last month, after 25 years of autonomous government, illustrates these problems.

In spite of some specific characters we would be able to conclude that the global institutional system of Spain is similar to the federalist ones, and we can distinguish two levels of government (State and Autonomous Communities) and two levels of law, guaranteed by the constitution.

II. The So-Called Differential Facts as the Second Axis of the Autonomous State

However, the assertion that the autonomous system of Spain has resemblance to a federal state must be considered as relative because, besides the characteristics similar to the federalism quoted above, it also possesses other especial notes that we could denominate "differential fact" of certain AACC.

Catalonia, the Basque Country and other AACC have specific cultural, social and political aspects which are different from most other AACC. The originality of the Spanish autonomous system lies in the fact that the constitution recognizes the elements which historically configured the personality of the different people of Spain, and which in former eras had been prohibited or scorned by the centralist state. The preamble of the constitution refers, in plural, to the "people of Spain ... their cultures and traditions, languages and institutions." Art. 2 Spanish Constitution (SC) has a twofold reference to the "nationalities and regions" that Spain is comprised of, which is an admission that the collective conscience of some of the peoples of Spain has a greater sense of belonging to their own community than others do. It means that Spain is, in turn, a nation made up of different nationalities, which means that the country is effectively a plurinational reality.

Throughout the constitution, other precepts make it possible for the Statutes of Autonomy to include elements which are clearly related to this differential fact: Art. 3 (local languages), Art. 141.3 and 4 (territorial organization), Art. 149.1.8 SC (special civil law), Art. 149.1.29 (autonomous police forces), DA 1ª SC (the historic rights of Navarra and the Basque Country) and DA 3ª SC (the Canary Islands' economic and fiscal regime). On the basis of these precepts, certain Statutes of Autonomy have included elements they deem to be part of their differentiated personality, as one can see in the following scheme.

GRAPH 2: THE DIFFERENTIAL FACTS OF AUTONOMOUS COMMUNITIES

Basque Country	**Catalonia**	**Galicia**
Financial arrangement; Internal territorial demarcations, including Parliament-Gov.; Official territorial language (Basque); Autonomous police force (Ertzanza).	Official territorial language (Catalan, greatest importance); Special civil law; Autonomous police force.	Territorial language; Civil law.

Navarra	Canary Islands	Balearic Islands
Financial arrangement; Traditional civil law; Police force.	Fiscal and economic regime; Government on each island (Cabildos).	Catalan language, Government on each island (Consell).

The recognition of these special elements varies across the different AACC, and even the same elements take on a different importance in each one because of their different ideological role. The term "differential fact" means, by way of conclusion, that certain AACC have a different historical and political personality.

Besides the symbolic dimension of the differential facts, its recognition takes legal effects on different levels. Firstly, the exercise of freedoms, for example the right to use the Catalan or other territorial language, which was prohibited under Franco. A second level, which goes much further, consists of the institutionalization of the content of the differential fact, for example, the introduction of Catalan into the educational system, the administration and the public communications media. Thirdly, the possibility that even state institutions mirror the differential fact such as the use of Catalan in the courts or in certain Senate debates.

III. The Distribution of Competencies

1. *Initial problems*

The distribution of competencies in Spain arises from the constitution, but it continues in the Statutes of Autonomy, because the first one establishes the competencies of the state and – at the same time – the maximum ceiling for the AACC, but each Statute fixes the competencies that correspond to its respective AC, according with the so called "available principle" (to make a free decision). The sum of the competency rules of the constitution and the Statute of Autonomy is denominated "block of constitutionality" in the jurisprudence of the Constitutional Court. The central idea is that the competencies are defined together by the constitution and the Autonomy Statute for every singular AC.

The constitution of 1978 initially permitted distinguishing two groups of AACC with different competencies, according to the procedure for approval of the Statute of Autonomy. The first group approved its Statute by a reinforced procedure which largely meant the will of the biggest self-government. They were the Basque Country, Catalonia and Galicia (some times called historic nationalities), but also Andalusia and Navarra, and two other AACC (Canaries and Valencian Community). They reached a superior level of self-government for different reasons. The second group followed an easier way of approving the Statute, that meant less interest in the autonomy and they reached a smaller amount of powers (maximum in Art. 148 SC). Therefore, 7 AACC enjoyed an important level of competencies and autonomy from the beginning, while the other 10 initially had a very inferior grade of self-government, although the constitution foresaw a possible increase later.

The difference of competencies between the two groups of AACC was initially remarkable. While the first group assumed legislative and executive competencies in fields of education, health, environment, etc. the other 10 AACC could not regulate these matters and they had to conform with the central state in agriculture, cattle raising, and craft, etc. The difference between the two groups of AACC not only rests in legislative powers, but also in great inequality of the respective administration, because for education and health one needs thousands of teachers and doctors. That required a huge administration that was greatly reduced in the AACC that lacked such competencies.

The existence of two groups of AACC with very different levels of competencies lasted until 1992 when the socialist and conservative parties made "political pacts over the autonomy." Then, the 10 AACC with lesser competencies came to have the same competencies as the other ones. In the following years they also received all the administrative means that equalized them with the other AACC. The equalization was legitimate and positive, but some AACC (especially those governed by nationalist parties) considered that it reduced their own importance, and they have criticized this equality between the AACC, because some are nationalities and others are only regions.

2. *The main categories of competencies*

In the first years the Constitutional Court dictated many sentences on competency conflicts, and that made the distribution of powers between the state and the AACC easier. The result is quite reasonable and more or less similar to the ones in other federal countries. The experience of these years allows to distinguish the competencies into four large categories: exclusive competencies of the state, concurrent competencies, shared competencies and exclusive competencies of the AACC.

GRAPH 3: GENERAL CATEGORIES OF COMPETENCIES

Exclusive Competencies of the AACC Agriculture and Cattle Raising, Tourism, Social Services, Hunt and Fishing, Trade and Consume, Industry, Town Planning.	**Exclusive Competencies of the State** Defense and Armed Forces, International Relations, Nationality, Alienage and Asylum, Foreign Commerce, Ordination of the Credit and Banking, External Health.	**Double or Parallel Exclusives** Exclusive of the state or of the AACC according the reach of the territory or juridical category of the public service – Railroads, Transport, Hydraulic Uses, Ports and Airports, Public Works, Museums and Libraries.
Concurrent Competencies (Basic-Development Act) General Ordination of the Economy, Education, Local Régime, Health, Credit and Funds of Saving, Public Administrations and Officials, Environment, Mass-Communication, Media.	**Shared Competencies** (Legislation-Execution) Labor Legislation, Mercantile and Penitentiary Legislation, Intellectual and Industrial Property Legislation, Legislation on Pharmaceutical Products.	**Other Kinds of Competencies** Cultural Activities, Appellation of Origin, Public Order.

The "exclusive competencies", as much for the state as for the AACC allow their holder to exercise all powers on the corresponding matter, that is to say, it grants legislative and executive power.

The competencies of the state are exclusive when the rules of Article 149 SC are not limited in their legislative or executives abilities. For example, "nationality, immigration, status of aliens and right of asylum" (number 2), "international relations" (number 3), "defence and Armed forces" (number 4), etc.

These competencies are enunciated in a generic way, without any limit of functions, and for that reason they require a very precise delimitation of the matter. For example, "international relations" means that it corresponds to the state the signature of international treaties or the establishment of embassies, but the AACC can carry out agreements with German Länder or Swiss Cantons in matters that correspond to them. Thus, we have arrived to distinguish between "international relations" of the state and "foreign action" of the AACC.

The exclusive competencies of the AACC allow them to exercise all the functions in legislation and execution. The autonomous exclusive competencies do not appear in the Article 149 SC, nor do they appear as exceptions of the reserved matters to the state. They are recognized by the Statute of Autonomy. Exclusive areas are, for example, agriculture and tourism (they do not appear in 149 SC, the special civil legislation of Catalonia and Navarra, that it is a part of differential acts (exception to the general civil law in number 8). There are different rights such as railroads or highways that we can call "parallel" or "double" because they are exclusive to the state or to the AC according to their layout.

The competence is concurrent (it is sometimes called "shared legislation") when the state must approve a basic law, settling only general norms, and the AACC can approve the development laws, and they also have regulation and execution powers. All the sections of the 149.1 SC that attribute to the state the basic legislation or the bases are concurrent competencies. Concurrent competencies apply in such important matters as general economy, education, health, and environment. The biggest difficulty with this kind of competence is to decide on the extension, the reach, of the bases approved by the state act. The Constitutional Court has fixed some approaches (they should contain the "minimum common denominator" for all citizens, they should be acts approved by parliament and only exceptional regulations, etc.) but there exist many conflicts.

"Shared competence" corresponds to the state the approval of legislation and executive regulation of them, to guarantee normative equality in the whole territory, and it corresponds to the AACC to approve the organizing regulation and the whole administration. Shared competencies exist in the mercantile and penitentiary legislation, as well as the labour legislation, that is maybe the most important one for the AACC.

Most of the competencies are registered in some of these four big categories, but with many different shades according to the matters; also, some competencies have particular rules like the appellation of origin that needs the agreement of the AC and the state. There are also three or four matters depending on one concrete act and not on the "constitutional block" like public order and police.

Some general principles also fall into the categories of competencies, especially when they affect the equality of citizens. In the autonomous state, like in some federal ones, a dialectic tension exists among the equality and the diversity of rights that it is not always easy to solve. The first number of Art. 149.1 SC attributes to the state the competence to regulate basic conditions that guarantee the equality of Spaniards in the exercise of rights and constitutional duties, in a similar way to "equivalent conditions of life" contained in the German constitution. On the other hand, the different treatment of citizens among AACC is limited by the discrimination that is forbidden by the Articles 138.2 and 139.1 SC, when the difference is unjustified or arbitrary and it means a privilege (Constitutional Sentences 61/1997 and 188/2001).

The constitution also foresees possibilities to make some competencies flexible. The general rule to modify competencies is the reform of the constitution or of the Statutes that are rigid. But, without arriving at this end, the constitution contains three mechanisms in order to modify one concrete competence (Art. 150): Framework-Act, Transfer Organic Act and Act for "harmonization" of the law. The technique most utilized, up to now, is the transfer organic law that allows the state to pass over a competence to one or several AACC.

IV. Criticism and Alternatives

Beyond the examined ordination of competencies, the state has spread its intervention to almost all social realities. In most cases, the state accepts the space of legislation and execution of the AACC but it superimposes a general mark of public policies politicians settled down in exercise of its own competencies.

This pre-eminence of the state maybe was implicit in the constitution, but the practice has confirmed and reinforced very much in the horizontal and vertical level of the competencies system. In the first, by way of an extensive interpretation of competencies in “general ordination of the economy” or in “commerce legislation”, etc. that bears the parallel reduction of the exclusive jurisdictions of the AACC in matters like agriculture, tourism, industry, etc. The exclusivity of the AACC goes downhill with regard to the state's sum of a plurality of competencies.

In the vertical "dimension" state competencies become clear mainly in the concurrent competencies, where it extends the space of the basic legislation and also dictates not only acts but also rules and even carrying out acts of mere execution.

In conclusion, a significant reduction of the reach of the exclusivity of the AACC has taken place and a correlative increment in extension and depth of the intervention of the state. The state has been able to act in almost all matters, not only in fixing big political guidelines, but also legislative options. On the other hand, the AACC has been able to legislate in wide material environments and they have become the ordinary administration of the big public services (health, teaching, etc.); however, their capacity to adopt own public policies has certainly been limited.

Those problems have been increased by the weakness of cooperation mechanisms among the state and the AACC that hinders the effective operation of the system and impels the state to look for centralized solutions; and also by the changes that derive from the integration of Spain in the European Union have benefited the state to the detriment of the AACC (there is a project to facilitate the autonomous participation in the elaboration of the communitarian decisions through the state).

The grade of normative detail which the state can use through the concurrent competencies reduces the capacity of the AACC to fix their own policies. The diagnosis made by a Catalan professor, *Carles Viver*, former Magistrate of the Constitutional Court and now director of the Catalan Institute has been spread, impelling the reform of the Statute of Autonomy: the political autonomy in Spain is wide, but of low quality. The AACC has attributed, it has already been said, an important executive function whose exercise bears, without a doubt, the exercise of an important power, but the political dimension of the autonomy has been devaluated notably.

To revise the concept and the reach of the basic legislation of the state, and to achieve a superior length of AACC, there are two lines, one more dogmatic and the other more institutional, with some points of coincidence. The first line, defended by professor *Viver* seeks to enlarge to the maximum the size of exclusivity of the AACC reducing all possible spaces of concurrence, by the subdivision of matters. The second line, that I consider a more realistic guaranty of autonomy, trusts in the reform of the Senate to be a similar Council to the *Bundesrat*. I know the current process of reform in Germany is trying to reduce the powers of the *Bundesrat*, but one must keep in mind that in Spain the AACC do not participate at all in the approval of concurrent laws. There are some points of coincidence between these positions: the most clear is the demand of character of formal laws of parliament to the norms falling into concurrent competencies, without accepting that the basic legislation is in regulations of the government. The other possible agreement would affect the compatibility of both lines, the shape of basic legislation as norms of principals and the participation of the AACC in its approval.

It would probably be easy to reach an agreement in Catalonia to change the character of some competencies, reducing the concurrence in areas like the local régime or the autonomous public function giving more power to the autonomy by the subdivision of these matters. It seems that this would be a tendency extended in some federalisms, for example in the new constitution of Switzerland, and maybe also in the debates of Germany.

Next to this quite academic debate, in the present intent of reform of the Statute of Catalonia there are other more political discussions, like the amplification of power of the AACC in the Courts of Justice or the attribution of competencies to the AACC that regard immigration, that seem a reasonable position. But there are other questions outlined by the most nationalist positions as the recognition of the self-determination right of nations or a fragmentation of the fiscal system (the so-called "Basque Financial Arrangement"), that seem less reasonable and even outside the constitutional limits.

In conclusion, as one can sense, the debate in Spain is complicated because the axis centralism-federalism (or political decentralization) face with other partially different that confront the general parties (of all Spain) to the nationalist parties of one Autonomous Community (Catalonian, Basque Country, etc.). The situation is a bit more complicated because reform needs the consensus of socialists with the conservative (and more centralist) party and because the Catalan government includes socialists (federalist) and radical nationalists, while other important nationalists are in parliamentarian opposition. Also, like in all decentralized states, the discussion must keep in mind the binomial development-solidarity.

But in any case, in the last 25 years we have reached a grade of remarkable self-government and this positive experience should serve us to advance, now in the new mark of the European Union, with more complexity but also with a wider horizon.

LIST OF PARTICIPANTS

Prof. *Eliseo Aja,* speaker, Professor for Constitutional Law, Director of the Institute for Public Law, University of Barcelona.

Prof. Dr. *André Alen*, speaker, Professor for Constitutional Law, Catholic University of Leuven; Judge at the Arbitragehof – Cour d'arbitrage (Belgian Constitutional Court).

Univ.-Doz. Dr. habil. *Peter Bußjäger,* speaker, Associate Professor at the Institute of Public Law, Financial Law and Political Science at the University of Innsbruck; Director of the Institute of Federalism, Innsbruck; Director of the Landtag Vorarlberg; member of the Austrian Convention.

Prof. Avv. *Beniamino Caravita di Toritto,* speaker, Professor for Public Law and Economic Law, University of Rome "La Sapienza".

Prof. *Arthur B. Gunlicks*, speaker, Professor of Political Science, University of Richmond, Virginia.

Prof. Dr. *Bernd von Hoffmann,* Professor of Civil, Comparative and Private International Law in Trier; 1992 Lectures Hague Academy of International Law Board, Board Institute for Legal Policy, Trier.

Elisabeth Kopp-Iklé, Minister of Justice (1984-1989), Switzerland.

Dr. *Hans W. Kopp,* speaker, Managing Partner Kopp & Partners, Zurich; President of the Federal Commission of Experts for a Global Mass Communication and Mass-Media Concept (1978-1984); lecturer at the University of Zurich (1963-1988); Master's Thesis at the University of Michigan Law School: Federalism and Taxation in the United States and Switzerland.

Prof. Dr. *Christine Langenfeld,* Professor of Public Law at the University of Göttingen.

Prof. *Jean Leclair,* speaker, Professor, Faculty of Law, Université de Montréal.

Mr. *Koen Muylle,* speaker, Assistant at the Institute for Constitutional Law, Catholic University of Leuven; Law Clerk at the Arbitragehof – Cour d'arbitrage (Belgian Constitutional Court).

Prof. Dr. *Francesco Palermo,* Director, Institute for Studies on Federalism and Regionalism, European Academy, Bolzano.

Dr. *Horst Risse,* speaker, Head of the secretariat of the Joint Bundestag and Bundesrat Committee on Modernisation of the Federal System, Bundesrat, Berlin.

Prof. Dr. *Gerhard Robbers,* Professor for Public Law at the University of Trier; Director of the Institute for European Constitutional Law and Director of the Institute for Legal Policy; Judge at the Administrative Court of Appeals Rhineland-Palatine.

Carolin Zwilling, Researcher at the European Academy of Bolzano (EURAC).

Rechtspolitisches Symposium
Legal Policy Symposium

Herausgegeben im Institut für Rechtspolitik an der Universität Trier
von Bernd von Hoffmann und Gerhard Robbers

Band 1 Bernd von Hoffmann (ed.): Towards a Common European Immigration Policy. Reports and Discussions of a Symposium held in Trier on October 24th and 25th, 2002. 2003.

Band 2 Bernd von Hoffmann (ed.): Global Governance. Reports and Discussions of a Symposium held in Trier on October 9th and 10th, 2003. 2004.

Band 3 Gerhard Robbers (ed.): Reforming Federalism – Foreign Experiences for a Reform in Germany. Reports of a Symposium held in Trier on December 2nd to 4th, 2004 hosted by the Institute for Legal Policy at the University of Trier in Cooperation with the German Bundesrat. 2005.

www.peterlang.de

Peter Lang · Europäischer Verlag der Wissenschaften

Bernd von Hoffmann (ed.)

Global Governance

Reports and Discussions of a Symposium held in Trier on October 9th and 10th, 2003

Frankfurt am Main, Berlin, Bern, Bruxelles, New York, Oxford, Wien, 2004.
199 pp., num. tab.
Legal Policy Symposium. Edited in the Institut for Legal Policy at the University of Trier by Bernd von Hoffmann and Gerhard Robbers. Vol. 2
ISBN 3-631-52770-5 / US-ISBN 0-8204-7325-1 · pb. € 39.–*

While stopping globalisation no longer seems to be a valid option, the task of shaping it has gained priority. But who can effectuate good global governance? The ability of international institutions to provide reliable international structures seems challenged by the recent developments in international politics. What are the implications of the war in Iraq for international law and future global policy? How can governmental and non-governmental actors frame global governance? And what are the prospects of global development policy? These complex questions can only be addressed effectively in an interdisciplinary forum. On October 9th and 10th, 2003, the Institute for Legal Policy at the University of Trier invited notable experts from the disciplines of law, political and economic science to discuss and reflect on these issues. This volume embodies the results of that interdisciplinary workshop on global governance.

Contents: The Status of Public International Law seen from a European Perspective · The UN's Irrelevant Relevance · Globalisation, Politics and the State · The United Nations as an Actor of Globalization · The Role of NGOs in Global Governance: Controlling Corruption – The Example of Transparency International · International Business needs International Rules · The Role of the WTO in Global Development Policy · Findings from the World Bank Corporate Governance Country Assessments · Is Globalisation Detrimental for Developing Countries? · Conclusions

Frankfurt am Main · Berlin · Bern · Bruxelles · New York · Oxford · Wien
Distribution: Verlag Peter Lang AG
Moosstr. 1, CH-2542 Pieterlen
Telefax 00 41 (0) 32 / 376 17 27

*The €-price includes German tax rate
Prices are subject to change without notice

Homepage http://www.peterlang.de